3-

murdering my youth

a memoir

Cady McClain

Cover Design: André Provedel
Cover photo: Courtney Lindberg

*This book is dedicated to those who listened
and did not judge.*

"The past is never dead. It's not even past."
William Faulkner

I have tried to recreate conversations, events, and locales from my memory of them. Some names and identifying details have been changed to protect the privacy of living individuals.

Warning: this book includes strong language, graphic depictions of child abuse, sexual abuse, and domestic violence. If you are a trauma survivor you may find yourself triggered. It is not my intention to sensationalize or provoke, but to seek understanding.

Contents

Sisters

Memory is a tricky thing. Sometimes trying to remember the past is like stabbing around in the dark with a penknife, trying to kill a monster. I have flickers of images that come to me as if they were illuminated by lightning, after which I am pitched back into the darkness—blind but full of feeling.

New York City is like that: elusive, breathtaking, vital. I love New York the most at night. In the dim light of the yellowed street lamps, one working, another not, the traffic lights ever changing from red to green—my future is always right next to me, not too far ahead, the past lost somewhere in the dark. It is then I feel as if I can finally inhabit the fullness of myself, dodging the angry drunks, stopping for the strange...

"Oh look, there's a man with a cat on his head!" Literally. He has a cat balanced on the top of his head. I stop and talk to him for a while, about the other animals he has at home, about his cat that has a funny name I can't remember. She is white with black spots and is very calm, very pleased to be sitting on this man's head.

The man with the cat on his head tells me some story of trouble and asks for a donation. I am happy to part with five bucks to ease his sorrow.

I was once told that everything worth having could be bought for five bucks. Why? Maybe because it's just enough and not too much, maybe because it's what my grandma used to send me in the mail for my birthday, or maybe because five bucks once bought treasure, a bounty for two small girls...

I was born in Los Angeles. When I was a toddler, my mother gave my sister Annie five dollars and said it was okay for us to go buy some candy by ourselves. Together we walked to a small store located a few blocks away. My sister was seven years old. I was four. We spent all the money Mom gave us, not thinking we were doing anything wrong. It was candy! Happiness! We rushed home to show her all the pretty chocolate bars we had bought. We thought she'd be as happy as we were. Instead when we showed her the bag, she flew into a rage. She poured the candy on the Formica-covered kitchen table and threw us into the wooden bent back chairs that surrounded it.

"I can't believe you spent it all! Well, you bought it, you eat it!" She was red-faced and furious. "All of it!"

We stared at her, dumbfounded.

"Eat it!" she commanded.

Fat tears choked me as I broke off chunks of a once joyous chocolate bar and put them in my mouth one by one, creating a new taste of bittersweet. I watched my sister fall into silence, as if she felt guilty for her part in what was happening, as if she should have known how our mother would react.

A few years earlier, the three of us had moved from a

large, brown two-story house where our parents were living after they were married, to a smaller, blue house a few blocks away after they separated. I had the feeling our mother was ashamed of this smaller house, even though we still had fruit trees, grass, and a nice backyard. I think it was because she was there without a husband. The first time my parents separated was about a year after I was born.

I have an image in my mind of my mom lying on her queen-sized bed with the TV on, totally fazed out. Her room back then was filled to overflowing by a large 1970's style wooden bed and dresser set—a set meant for a larger room in a larger house for a larger life. Her small black and white TV was almost always on. She would lie there for hours.

I stayed in my room and waited for her to want me, obsessing about her sometimes, other times lost in the sensory distractions that make up most of the life of a visually challenged toddler—gauzy sheets, hazy summers, and bright colors. When she finally did get up, I never knew whether she'd be in a bad mood or wanting to be silly and play.

My mother's name was Jacqueline Dana, but she went by Dana for most of our childhood, inexplicably switching to Jacquie for a while when we moved to the East Coast. Like me, she was born in California, but her parents moved to Moline, Illinois, when she was a baby. There her language was flavored with Midwestern sayings like, "Open mouth, insert foot." She liked that one a lot. There were others such as: "Use it or lose it; you'll look funny without it," "Drive it or park it," "Shit or get off the pot," and "Who died and left you boss?"

These and more were all heard in our house, but our mom

took it a step further. She thought it was hilarious to tell us, "Love each other, little sisters, because some day Mommy will be dead and gone, and all you'll have left is each other." She intended to make us behave, but instead this statement made me cry hysterically, which she found really annoying. When I wouldn't stop wailing, she put me in the car with the engine on and left me there. Apparently, that shut me up.

Our father, William McClain Jr., or Bill, was also born in California. He probably would have been happiest as a cowboy, but his ambition was too big for the Western life. Instead he got into politics, eventually working for Barry Goldwater Jr. He was very handsome, especially in a suit. I think he liked to pretend he was "Bond, James Bond", but the hard truth was he was not so bright. He was more like, "Pyle, Gomer Pyle."

A few years ago, I discovered a Los Angeles newspaper among my mom's memorabilia. On the front page was an article about a plane crash Dad and Barry Jr. barely survived. They had flown their small twin-engine Cessna into some telephone wires and landed nose down. The engine was pushed back into my father's lap, breaking his leg. Miraculously, his penis survived. My mom said he was drunk when it happened. Another photo shows him visiting the wreckage: head wrapped in gauze as he leans on a cane, leg in a cast. His expression is debonair, almost carefree. There was no sign of concern he had almost died, leaving a wife and two children without a provider.

When I was five years old, our parents decided to reconcile. They sold the little blue house in Los Angeles in exchange for a new home in Orange County—a place called Laguna

Niguel, about an hour-and-a-half south of the city, next to a surfing village called Dana Point. My sister and I were sent to a school nearby, located on the top of a small hill from which we could see the Pacific Ocean. Sometimes I could even see dolphins, leaping up in groups as they traveled south toward Mexico (looking for some good fish tacos, no doubt, but who isn't?) It felt clean and safe there, a good place to be a little girl. As I walked home from school, I could hear the eucalyptus trees gently whooshing, telling me, "Everything here is as it should be," and "we are a peaceful family of trees." The immediacy of nature lay upon my hair and skin like a soft balm, caressing me until the noise at home grew too loud for even nature to shush.

One day I stood on a wall of large fieldstones in our backyard so my mom could take pictures of me. The day was warm and sunny, around 76 degrees. The flowering bushes on the hill behind me moved softly, unsettled by my back pressing up against them. I wore an outfit my mother had made: an orange gingham dress replete with matching bonnet, petticoat, and lace trim. The night before she had set my light blonde hair in foam and plastic rollers, which fell around my face in bouncy curls when she took them out.

My scalp still hurt from the pulling. She had painted circles of red lip paint on my gently sweating cheeks, applying false eyelashes and red lips drawn in the shape of a heart to give me the look of a porcelain doll. My heart pounded as she held my face to examine her work. She didn't touch me softly.

Her black and silver Rolleiflex camera hung around her neck from a thin leather strap. Gold earrings in the shape of twisted ropes hung from her stretched earlobes around her short, curly dark brown hair—hair so unlike mine, the blonde child wonder. I wondered why she was torturing me this way. Was it because we looked so different? Did she believe I liked being put on display?

"Do something, Kate," she directed. "C'mon, pose!"

I smiled like a jack-o'-lantern and put my index finger to my chin as I had seen done somewhere before, probably on a TV show. I watched so much television that the stories and images blurred together—up to six hours a day, sometimes. A girl put her finger under her chin and curtsied for the gentleman caller in Westerns, right? Or was it in the movie musicals? I must have seen it on TV, or how would I have known to do it?

My sister lurked somewhere nearby. I sensed her but didn't see her. It wasn't safe to take my eyes off our mother. Annie suddenly sneezed dramatically. Allergies. They were an excellent excuse not to participate in our mother's whims.

"Go inside," barked our mom. "You look sick."

As Mom fiddled with her camera, I quickly glanced over and watched my older sister retreat into the house. Her sharp eyes glared at us through the screen door. In that moment I thought she was a coward, that she should be the one on the wall catching these flaming arrows of rage coming out of our mother. But I hadn't been smart enough to come up with a good excuse. I had to take the full brunt of it. I reasoned that if I did whatever my mother wanted me to in that moment, perhaps she would show mercy later.

She wanted me to smile.

I smiled.

Snap, snap went the camera lens. Snapping off pieces of me. Pressing my tiny body onto film so Mom would feel like an artist and no longer like a frustrated housewife who needed to drink late into the night. I took a flower from the bush behind me and pulled it toward my nose. My other hand reached back, fingers lifted toward the sky like a Balinese dancer.

"Oh, love the rose, yes do that."

Snap, snap.

She was happy so I was happy, or so I thought. I could bend myself easily then, to be what she wanted me to be.

Since childhood, my sister Annie could control her thoughts and emotions if she was deeply engrossed in a book. Her room was filled with bookshelves lined with little girls' fantasy fiction—the Nancy Drew series, the *Little Women* series, *Pride and Prejudice, Alice in Wonderland, The Secret Garden,* and *The Diary of Anne Frank.*

Inspired by these books, she turned our toy dolls and stuffed animals into a sophisticated hierarchy. "The Queens" were two dolls with hoop skirts and big hairdos that stood high and imperious in bright pink and purple gowns on the top of a bookcase. Annie decided they were the ones in charge, and they would essentially scold or care for the other dolls and stuffed animals down below. Tough but fair, Annie would make them nod knowingly at each other when a commandment was justly given. Every other stuffed animal or doll was given a place in the hierarchy and public duty, which she then catalogued on multi-colored index cards in her best handwriting. "Princes" and "bishops" governed while "doctors" and "teachers" helped the "common people." "Crossing guards" and "bus drivers" (stuffed bears and long-eared plush rabbits) served in caps and jackets, and "The Rabble" (or rattier "stuffies") kept things interesting by misbehaving.

Most of my stuffed animals were "The Rabble." I loved them deeply and slept with them all around me in a circle, so they could protect me in the middle of the night. They had a chewed-on, hard-loved look and I liked that. I liked them to be punchy and fun, to make them get into lots of trouble so Annie's "Queens" would have something to do. Deep down, I believed all the dolls and animals were good, as were we, as was the whole kingdom. I made sure "Teddy" and "Big Dog" would hug each other and forgive any slight at the end of the play day.

After one of our games, our mother came tearing into our childhood rooms, throwing open the closets. She pulled out all the clothes, shoes, and toys stuffed inside, throwing everything on the floor. Then she did the same with our chests of drawers. *Open. Dump. Open. Dump.* Eventually the room was filled with little colorful mountains, stars, hearts, and bears tossed together in a mad kaleidoscope of baby dreams.

"Pick it up!" She screamed, "Pick up your goddamn mess!"

We did as we were told.

By the time I was seven years old, it was clear I had developed a lisp. In order for me to practice my "S's and R's," Mom decided she would use an old Greek technique for practicing one's speech, only she would do it "Dana Style." She placed two of her unused tampons inside my mouth, one on each side, stuffed between my cheeks and teeth.

"Like Demosthenes used pebbles!" she stated, proud of

her totally insane idea.

I stood in the middle of the study—the strings of her supersized tampons hanging out of the corners of my mouth and down my chin as the consonants came out "Ehth, ehsh, awr, awhr." I already knew what the tampons were for—they were supposed to be put inside one's lady parts. As much as I tried to ignore this fact and enunciate, tears burned down my face as my eyes begged her to stop the humiliation. She just stood there with her tumbler full of Scotch and laughed her ass off.

While surviving my mother's whims and rages was challenging, my dad managed to confuse the hell out of me on a whole other level. When I was eight years old, in the fourth grade, he molested me in my parents' bedroom. It started something like this:

One afternoon my mother announced, "Annie and I are going to the store. Stay with your father. We'll be back in a couple hours."

"Okay," I replied, feeling especially small in my blue jean shorts and stained Snoopy t-shirt. I held onto my soccer ball and felt bad. They'd probably get ice cream and not bring me one. I thought perhaps I had hurt Mom's feelings somehow. I did like Dad better. He was nicer to me most of the time. Nicer than he was to Annie for some reason. My sister glared at me silently. She took the brunt of his judgmental comments but seemed to hate our father for other reasons, too. Reasons she kept to herself. I knew she saw my love for him as a betrayal of her feelings.

"What are we going to do, Dad?" I asked after the door shut behind them.

"Let's take a nap." He was already drunk. "It's Sunday. I'm tired."

An afternoon nap was usually something my parents did together, so it seemed pretty special I was being asked to take part in this weekly ritual. I ran to my parents' bedroom and threw myself on the bed while my dad pulled the curtains. Then we both lay down and fell asleep.

At first it was nice to nap with my dad. I loved him, after all.

It was maybe a half hour later that I became aware that something was very wrong with my daddy that day. He had forgotten where he was. He was reaching out to me in a way I couldn't understand—except I knew I wasn't supposed to understand, at least not yet.

He started by kissing me on the mouth. I knew he was drunk so I said, "Daddy, no." Still he kept kissing. Then he rolled on top of me and began to rub his penis against me. I knew it was his penis because I had seen it in the shower, but it was hard now, it was pressing against my tummy and below, and it hurt.

"Daddy, no."

His hands roamed around my body and I started to feel aroused, which terrified me. I did not understand what was happening. I remember thinking, "What am I supposed to do? How do I not hurt his feelings? What is happening?" A flurry of thoughts, like paper in a storm, flashed through my mind.

He was kissing me like he kissed Mom.

"Daddy, no. Daddy…no. Daddy, no."

After that I remember nothing. Only fragments. I think I

pushed him off. I think I left the room. I don't remember. I've tried. I simply can't.

During an afternoon that had meant nothing more to anyone than a Sunday with the kids, to my child's mind my father became my lover, whether or not his penis went inside me. For days and weeks afterwards, I couldn't think straight. My thoughts sounded like this: "Daddy didn't mean to do wrong. He loves me, he wouldn't hurt me, and I love him." I thought this passionately, defensively. "Besides, it's Mommy who is the crazy one, always screaming and yelling and throwing all the clothes on the floor. My Daddy loves me—maybe just a little too much. He loves me and he was showing me that love. I just wasn't ready for it; that was all."

I thought about the other girls at school. Did they have a relationship like this with their father? I doubted it, but it was hard to know for sure. It wasn't something I could just come out and ask on the playground or while picking up my milk in the cafeteria. I started to watch the other children carefully for signs but everyone looked sparkling, as if they had been wiped down with Windex before they left the house. I doubted they could guess at my father's way of showing love. I wished I had the same bottle of cleaner they had, so I could be sparkling again.

There were so many smaller yet still inappropriate sexual moments in our house it's impossible to list them all. For example, he and Mom thought it was fun to take showers with us. My sister and I would giggle and cling to each other with nerves as they soaped us up. We tried not to look at our parents' genitals but they were right at our eye line and hard to miss. Then there was the time that Dad rented a boat. Once we were out on the ocean, we all had to take off our clothes. Annie hated this. She was a pre-teen then and becoming aware of her changing body. Later I wondered why we were naked together as a family so much. Was it some 1970's thing or did our dad need us all to know that he had a penis and we didn't? Sometimes even the way he hugged me felt strange, as if he didn't quite know how to touch a girl who wasn't a woman yet. Another time he did yoga naked in the middle of the living room. When he did his handstand, his hairy balls hung upside down for all the world to see.

We interrupt this moment for a word from our sponsor:

When I returned to All My Children in 2011 for the ending of the network series, I encountered an old friend in the makeup room. He was telling a story to everyone about how he liked to walk around naked in front of his children.

"We think it's good for them. We don't want them to have shame about their bodies, so we walk around with no clothes on sometimes. It's natural."

This particular actor had a tendency to enjoy shocking people with his outrageous stories. I could tell that his desire to put the hair and makeup department into a state of embarrassed silence was working. I was no longer one to back down from a dare, so I piped in.

"Seriously? You walk around naked in front of your kids?"

"Yeah, we don't want them to feel shame about their bodies. Hey, maybe when they are grown up, their boyfriends won't measure up, heh heh, but you know. They gotta' know what it's supposed to look like."

I shook my head. This guy needed straightening out. "Listen to me, man. My parents walked around naked." The room got quieter. I could feel heads straining to hear our conversation. "My dad did yoga naked in the living room." The room was now silent. "Dude, I've had sixteen years plus of therapy. Trust me when I tell you a pair of upside down balls and a flaccid cock is not something a six-year-old should be regularly staring at."

He looked at me for a moment, a somewhat amused expression on his face. I continued.

"Do you want this," I pointed at myself, "to happen to <u>your</u> kids?"

He paused, took me in, and with absolute perfect timing replied, "You have a point."

Love and Marriage

My parents met in San Francisco in 1963. Mom was a secretary and Dad was a typewriter salesman. Instead of marching, protesting, or dancing in the streets, Dana and Bill holed up in her apartment and made love as if their screwing was turning the world on its axis—when they were really only wearing down the mattress and each other.

My dad bought a little Austin Healey, and together they drove up and down the California coast like a poor man's Cary Grant and brunette Grace Kelly. Young and free, Bill was the kind of man who wanted to get his pilot's license and fly around the world. Although she liked some adventure, Dana wasn't as comfortable with his idea of what constituted a good time. She believed what many women still do—that kids and a house and the steady, normal routine of family life would heal the wounds of their pasts and make life better. Two weeks after they met each other, he proposed to her on the bluffs overlooking the Pacific Ocean.

After marrying in San Diego, they took their honeymoon

in Todos Santos, a tiny Mexican beach town in Baja, just south of the border. There they swam and lay on the beach. The hotel owners made a wedding cake for them. As a joke, my dad took my mom to a whorehouse in Tijuana. He thought it was funny. She didn't.

Her own words, words I found written on the back of a photograph, say it best: "Still there were signs even then I should have problems in the future—but I was young and in love and glossed over them."

My father's mother, Katherine, was born in the Guadalupe Valley in northern Baja, Mexico, where my great-grandparents grew flowers for a living. (I am part Mexican on my father's side.) Katherine was an artist who painted and took photographs, mostly documenting the natural world around her. According to all who knew her, she was a kind, sensitive woman.

My grandfather was a handsome Scotch-Irish cattle rancher, and by all accounts, an alcoholic. He fell in love with Katherine and had one child—my father. They made due in a one-room shack north of the border in El Cajon, using a curtain to create a bedroom. Outside, they grew vegetables, raised livestock, and drove cattle. I heard no stories of fighting, but Katherine died very young, when my dad was eleven, from stomach cancer. My father started drinking not long after that.

Alcohol caused a lot of problems in our house. The fights were loud and terrible and peppered with Spanish. Mom had picked up a few words to communicate with him more effectively, but they wouldn't teach it to us for some reason. My guess is they liked having a secret language to themselves, but I wonder if they were also a tiny bit ashamed of him being related to people south of the border—people with different shades of skin who knew what real poverty looked like.

"Goddamn it, Bill! Bastardo! How are we going to pay for the house now? Selfish cabron! Va chingate!"

When the fights got really bad, Mom would shove us girls into the car and announce that we were "going to Grandma's," which meant her mother's house in Moline, Illinois. These cross-country drives happened at least once a year. Sometimes we made it all the way there but not always. It was a long drive with little money to pay for gas or food. I recall one particular trip where we only had a bag of oranges to eat.

"If you're hungry, grab an orange," was our mother's decree. "They fight scurvy!"

I didn't know what scurvy was, but I didn't want to get yelled at so I ate those oranges up and tried to be happy about it.

Mom happened to be having her period one trip. She dried her used tampons on the back dashboard of the car on a paper towel so we wouldn't have to spend the gas money on Tampax. I remember watching those small brown fingers of cotton as they rolled back and forth, but I couldn't for the life of me remember what they were for. Annie remembered and had to sit in the back seat. She moved as far away from them as possible and said nothing.

When we finally arrived at our grandmother's white Cape Cod style house, she would without question be tootling around in a pink silk housecoat smelling like a combination of whiskey and rose body powder. After hours of driving we gathered in her perfectly preserved 1950's kitchen to eat ladyfingers, dipping them into port wine from tall crystal glasses. My sister and I sat and listened to the two women laughing hysterically for hours, soaking up her hospitality like the ladyfingers in the wine.

Our mother's parents had not made it for the long haul. After many years of marriage, hard work, and children, Grandfather had decided to explore his lifelong dreams of adventure. Unfortunately for Grandma, he had gone off with his secretary to partake in them. She hadn't handled it particularly well. My guess is she lost her will to fight. Exit self-esteem; enter pink housecoat, wry humor, and whiskey.

Sharing laughter at men's folly was one thing. Sharing defeat was another. Our mom could see she was becoming a mirror of her mother—wearing her bathrobe too long into the day at home and leaning hard on the booze to "take the edge off." In order to avoid falling into the same pattern, Mom would load us back into the car to return to "that asshole" and "make it work."

The drive home was always more pleasant than the drive to Illinois. Perhaps because it was full of hope. I loved driving through the desert, watching the colorful, wide-open skies as tiny stars began to randomly appear. I would twist the radio dial, searching for a station that was playing a familiar song so I could sing out loud to it, which Mom liked.

"Mirrors on the ceiling and pink champagne on ice. We are all just prisoners here of our own device..."

When we finally returned home, Mom would use the phone to track Dad down, threatening desperate acts if he didn't return immediately from wherever he was. Then she would drink and wait while my sister and I tidied up around the house singing Disney songs. Annie and I liked to pretend there were little birds and animals helping us clean, like in the cartoons and movies we saw on television.

"If you say it loud enough, it always sounds precocious," we would holler over the sound of the vacuum. "Supercalifragilisticexpialidocious!"

Eventually "that asshole" would make his appearance: stiff, angry, and a little drunk. The two of them would then shack up in the bedroom for hours—Mom only coming out in her robe to make sure us girls had food and TV.

After a few days of reconciliation, another show of family would begin, with Dad building a new fence, planting bushes, or some other job Mom thought he'd be good at. She'd pretty herself up for dinner with brown eyeliner and coral lipstick, putting on her gold hoop earrings and drawing in her eyebrows. Instead of watching TV we'd sit in the fancy chairs at the dining table as Mom served up her latest recipe from *Sunset* magazine. Annie and I sat quietly for as long as we could, but we liked to hum when we ate. This amused our father until it didn't. "You're disgusting," he would say, silencing us with a sharp verbal jab to the heart.

After a couple of weeks, everything returned to the same stuck place: the fights about money, other women, bills, "you promised" and "I never." Annie and I would lie together under her bed while our parents exhausted themselves with another bilingual showdown. Huddled in our flowered pajamas, we sometimes pretended strangers had kidnapped us for an enormous ransom and plotted our grand escape. I often wondered what would have happened if Annie and I had just crawled out the window, leaving the two savages that called themselves "parents" to work it out without an audience. I remember staring out that window at the world beyond, knowing it would only take a bag and a moment. However, when I thought about the coyotes, the strangers, and the blackness beyond, I was grateful for my spot under the bed.

Instead of crawling out the window, I would think about my dad. He didn't mean to be cruel or to confuse me with Mom. He loved me, maybe even more than he loved her. I imagined him and me hanging out together on a beach somewhere, listening to the waves—a couple of pirates escaping the real world.

"Hey monkey," my dream father would mumble over a plastic cup of Scotch with ice that softly thudded like a boat against a buoy, safe at harbor.

"Hey Daddy," I would say back, smiling and clinging to his arm or leg, happy for the smallest connection, happy to feel safe from my mother's rages.

This moment never happened.

A woman friend of mine had a grand mal seizure recently and woke up remembering absolutely nothing about who she was or where she came from.

"I couldn't remember a thing for hours. It was like I had no history," she said, a dreamy expression on her sweet Swedish face. "I was so happy. I felt absolutely wonderful."

I've been thinking about this statement for some time now. What would it mean to have no memory? Would I be a hap-

pier person? "Most definitely," I think, initially. But then who would I be without my past? Nature has created our minds so that experience creates permanent physical grooves in our brain in order to help us survive. Our past is why we might have the instinct to look both ways before we cross the street, the impulse to say "thank you," when someone helps us get up after a fall, and for some, a heightened reaction to another person's needs. Many times in my life, I have wished I could de-program this ingrained compulsion in my head—the desire to fix what I instinctively feel is broken in another.

Like No Business I Know

"I've got money, Mom. You can have it!"

Our parents opened accounts for my sister and me at Bank of America. It was a special program for kids called "The Squirrel's Club." It was supposed to be a way for children to practice saving and investing by depositing the money Grandma sent in a flowery birthday card or earned from selling lemonade. Found nickels and dimes were literally "squirreled away," but it never grew much. In desperate moments, our parents would cash them out and use the money to help pay off the gas or electric bill—whatever wasn't getting covered that month because Dad had drunk away his paycheck.

Our mom was desperate for a solution to our constant debt, but it seemed that taking a job was not in the cards for her, even though she had graduated from law school. Instead, she focused on trying to make our father into a better lawyer. His lack of ethics seemed to be at odds with his chosen profession, however, and soon he was asked to leave his firm. The tension in the house was palpable. When I made Mom or Dad smile, the tension stopped for a moment.

This is how performers are made.

After a fellow student punched me in the stomach for no particular reason, my mom put me in tap and karate classes. Perhaps she figured I might develop some kind of Gene Kelly "dance and punch" moves. I worked hard in this class and "fa-lap, ball-change-ed" my little patent leather tap shoes right to the front of the class. This tiny show of talent gained the attention of one of my teachers. She had helped organize a stunt where hundreds of dancers of all ages would cover a football field in Anaheim, dancing in unison to the same routine. If all went well, it would be logged in the Guinness Book of World Records. The whole spectacle was to be filmed for live television. She invited me to join and, begging my Mom's permission, I did. Being one of the youngest and smallest dancers, on the day of the event, I was placed in the front row where the TV cameras would see me. It was so exciting—the lights, the crowd of people, the feeling of being involved in something that felt so important. It made me forget for a moment about the fights and the money and the weird afternoon with Dad.

That year, 1977, there were only three networks to watch on television, and I had been seen on one of them, right after the six o'clock news. Impressed, our neighbors next door called to find out how I ended up on the program. One girl in my fifth grade class displayed a jealousy I was about to see a lot more of at school.

She said, "You think you're something, but you're not!"

I looked at her squinty eyes and thought, "What's wrong with you? I'm on TV!" But her words cut deep. Hadn't I done something special? Hadn't I earned it?

Soon after the dance event aired, I heard that a girl in my tap class had done a television commercial, and I was instantly jealous. She was where I wanted to be: the happy place! I imagined the smiling crew, the bright lights, the music, and the fun of the Guinness World Record experience and thought if only I could do that all the time, then nothing else would matter. Nothing else would hurt.

I told my mom about it immediately.

"I want to do commercials, too!"

"Why, Kate?"

"Please? It's okay...my childhood is over!"

She looked at me like I was nuts.

Why she never questioned that statement, I can only guess. If she had asked, if she had dug deeply and explored why I felt that way, then she would know the truth and would have to acknowledge that she was a part of that truth. She would have to pay attention to the fact she was regularly denying her own child the right to be a child. It was now my request—not her dressing me up and putting me on stage. But I was nine years old. What the hell did I know? I just wanted to be where families smiled while passing hot, buttered, Pillsbury Powdered Buttermilk Biscuits; where children laughed and waved at the Kool-Aid dude (Oh yeah!); where moms bonded with their daughters by saying, "Shout it Out!" to stains on their t-shirts; and that all happened on TV.

As a way for me to get some more acting experience, my mom signed me up for an audition for *The Music Man* at a local community college. I got a small part in the chorus. We spent hours at the theater waiting for my turn to rehearse with a group of kids who were to follow the lead actor around singing, "Oh, oh, the Wells Fargo Wagon is a' coming round the bend, oh please, let it be for me!" while looking at one another in frenzied excitement. Afterwards we always went for ice cream with hot chocolate sauce that made us have to poop like crazy an hour after eating it.

Sometimes my sister was dragged along to my rehearsals because Mom didn't like leaving her at home with Dad during the summer. She was about eleven at that time and had just been sent away for her first year at boarding school to get her away from our father's random attacks of verbal cruelty. Annie watched me from the seats with a sarcastic expression that said everything but, "You are such an idiot." Who could blame her? I had taken center stage in our family, and it wasn't always pleasant for her. I truly believed what I was doing was going to save us all. If everyone had to stop fighting for a minute to watch me sing and dance, wasn't that a good thing?

Backstage before the show one night, Mom took pictures of me for my first headshot. In preparation, she applied my stage makeup: giant painted-in eyebrows, shadow, false eyelashes, and red lipstick. She pulled my ponytails way up high and curled them with a hot iron. Then she had this horrifying picture printed in black and white on glossy paper with my full name on it: "Katie Jo McClain." To make matters worse, the photo studio screwed up and printed the picture in reverse. She sent this disturbing photo out with my shortest of short resumes.

One agent called. Iris Burton.

Iris was a middle-aged New Yorker who had planted

herself in Southern California to make a hard but serious buck. Her specialty was child actors. Over the years she handled some very famous clients: River and Joaquin Phoenix, Fred Ward, Henry Thomas, Kirsten Dunst, Mary Kate and Ashley Olsen, Kirk Cameron, Drew Barrymore, Tori Spelling, and later Dakota and Elle Fanning. When she died in 2008, the New York Times quoted her to have said about her young clients, "I hate to say it, but kids are pieces of meat. I've never had anything but filet mignon. I've never had hamburger. My kids are the choice meat."

The first time I met her, she said three things:

"Lemme see your teeth, honey."

"Your ponytails are too high. Pull 'em down."

"Neva' wear that shirt again."

She was also quoted to have said, "By the time a kid walks in the door, I can tell if he or she's a winner or a loser. If they jump in or slouch in, if they're biting their nails or rockin' back and forth, I don't want 'em. If I don't see the hidden strength, feel the energy, then the magic isn't there. I can smell it like a rat."

I guess I should feel pleased that her nose smelled some "hidden strength and energy" in me but looking back, I wish my mother had seen what a monster this woman was and had run for the hills (taking a job there). Instead, we were grateful to have been one of the chosen and felt a strong obligation to live up to this woman's expectations.

My new agent was more than happy to call every other day with another audition for Tide or Mattel Toys. There was sometimes even an audition for a TV show or a movie—mediums I wasn't equipped to handle but didn't feel I had a choice about taking. If Iris called, you went. You were in or out.

Getting a job became a matter of showing up, luck, and mileage. Los Angeles, where all the auditions were held, was about an hour-and-a-half drive from our house in Laguna Beach. Mom started driving me up after school about three or four times a week. Having endured the cross-country trips, to me, these jaunts were a piece of cake. Pleasing the casting directors and producers wasn't too much of a stretch, either. I smiled when they wanted me to smile, said what they wanted me to say, and let them touch and turn me just like Mom did when she was getting me ready for a photo.

My first paying job was a national commercial for Band-Aids. I was to stand in front of a horse (with my ponytails squarely in the lower quadrant of my head) and sing the "I am stuck on Band-Aids" song.

"I am stuck on Band-Aids Brand, while Band-Aids stuck on me!"

I was to sing this catching ditty while washing a horse with a sponge. The checks this commercial brought in were outrageous—in less than a year, I was making more than my dad.

My parents were quick to capitalize on my sudden income. Since they were both familiar with the law, they decided to "incorporate" me, making me president of my own LLC (Limited Liability Corporation) at age nine. Through this corporation, they paid the mortgage on our house and took salaries for themselves as treasurer and secretary. My father bought himself new recording equipment for his office, and my mother a new TV for the living room. They were apparently unfamiliar with the Coogan Law—named after child actor Jackie Coogan—put into place in 1939 to protect child actors from having their earnings spent by their parents. If they were familiar...I...I try to believe that they broke that law out of sheer desperation.

I went on hundreds—possibly thousands—of auditions. Iris told us the going average for getting a job was one audition out of fifty. No matter how bad you were, if you just kept going, you were pretty much guaranteed to book the fiftieth audition. This was supposed to be encouraging.

Every audition had the same setup: I would find the waiting area for actors; sign the "sign in" sheet with my name, age, and social security number; fill in my agent's name and phone number; have my picture taken with a Polaroid camera (smile!) and have it attached to my "size card," which stated my height, weight, and basic measurements. Then I picked up and practiced my "sides," which were drawn pictures of the camera shots the clients had agreed on and the lines the actors were supposed to say. Once inside the casting office, I would stand in front of a video camera and state my name and age, sometimes turning around in a circle so they could see the full 360° of me. I was told never to forget that the cereal—not me—was the star of the show. My job was to sell the hell out of it. I did commercials for Mattel toys, Buster Brown shoes, McDonald's, Burger King, Pillsbury, Kool-Aid, Shout detergent, and many more.

Every job I booked meant more money. More money meant more "happy mommy and daddy." When the job was over, I would get a treat, like a giant ice cream sundae at Swenson's. When the check came, I was allowed to buy myself something I really wanted—some records or some stickers. One time I bought a giant four-foot teddy bear.

Theatrical auditions were more difficult. I didn't understand acting. It didn't feel the same as pretending to be a happy kid for a commercial, or playing with my sister at home. Despite this, I was cast in my first theatrical part when I was ten years old. It was for the film *My Favorite Year*, directed by Richard Benjamin. I was to play the part of "Tess Swann," the daughter of movie star and alcoholic "Alan Swann." The part of "Alan" was to be played by Peter O'Toole. There were no lines. I just had to be able to ride a bike. Sounded easy enough to me—too easy.

I remember the lighting in the room where I met the director and casting director was dim and the furniture plush and solid. It felt good to be in that cool, dark room with those kind people. Something about it softened me. Since I had no lines to perform, they just asked me about my life. I don't recall what I said, but apparently they were very pleased with it, whatever it was.

When Mom got the call from Iris telling us I had been hired to play Tess Swann, I felt as if I had been tapped on the shoulder and recognized for having some kind of greatness in me. It was kind of embarrassing. I knew the truth. I was just a kid being a kid.

My scenes were shot in Brentwood, a rich suburb of Los Angeles, which was standing in for Connecticut. (In the movies, production companies almost never shoot exactly in the location audiences believe they are in. It's part of the charm of The Business and how a production saves money.) The weather was gray on the day we shot my scene, which the crew seemed happy about. It made the light even and soft.

In the script, a movie star (played by O'Toole) arrives via chauffeured limo to visit his little girl (me), whom he hasn't seen in a long while. When he sees his child riding her bike up the street, he is filled with regret for not having been a better father and is unable to get out of the car. They had already shot the first part of me riding my bike and the car pulling around the bend and stopping. Mr. O'Toole's close-up was next. Simple.

What was not simple was Peter O'Toole. He had holed up in his trailer. I heard whispers from the crew (and my mother) that he was drunk.

As we all waited for what felt like an eternity for him to come out of the trailer, I remember thinking about how wonderful it would be to live in a big white house in Connecticut with a rich movie star dad. Everything in Brentwood/Connecticut seemed so perfect. The manicured lawn and the nice cars in the driveway emanated a sense of safety and security—nothing like the stress of our little Laguna house.

Interrupting my reverie, Mr. O'Toole emerged theatrically from his trailer. He was the tallest, thinnest, most weathered looking man I'd ever seen. He stopped, looked around, and then starting walking right in my direction. Once he arrived by my side, he hovered, not saying a word. He just smiled down at me. I could feel the crew holding their breaths. There was something about him—some kind of incredible energy. Then he unexpectedly put his hand on my head and began to stroke my hair. He did that for about a minute or two, then walked away.

After they got his close-up, I recall a murmur going

around that he was "brilliant...heartbreaking...magical...a genius." Then (of course) it was my turn. As his car pulled away in the shot and I rode my bike to my mark, all I could think was, "That was my dad. My magical dad who is supposed to love me and he just drove away." How the casting director knew that Peter O'Toole and I would have this strange connection I cannot say.

"And cut!"

The atmosphere on the set was very respectful of this moment—very respectful of me. I will always be grateful to Richard Benjamin for honoring me and creating a safe place where I could share what I was actually living. He didn't pinch me so I'd cry or ask me to make a tear roll down my cheek. He just let me be.

Sharing in this way did not hurt me at the time. It was more like walking into another paradigm. I cannot tell you how many years I wanted to walk back into that moment once it was over. That is the seduction and the curse of the movie business. Once you believe the imaginary world is even the tiniest bit real, you have lost a part of yourself, and the celluloid (or digital now) owns that part forever.

People have asked me why I didn't go back to L.A. to pursue a bigger career after I worked on *All My Children* for a few years, like most actors do. I shrug and tell them, "I was born there, I grew up there," which seems to suffice, but it's only part of the truth. The truth is I was traumatized by my acting experiences as a child and an adolescent in L.A. I had been hit on by producers, kissed by TV stars, and fondled by directors. Even if they didn't touch me, the lecherous stares from adult men could bring a blush to my face. I was "fresh meat" in Hollywood.

It is no fun being shark chum.

When I was fifteen years old, I had a callback for a film. It was being held at the director's house, a practice that wasn't all that unusual in Los Angeles—a city where there are more houses than office buildings. The director wanted me to come to the cottage in the backyard to meet with the producer and a male actor he was considering for a role. I was told the director wanted to see if we "had chemistry." Since it was a big opportunity and I wanted to look like a grown up, my mom waited in the car, parked outside on the road.

In the audition scene I had to kiss a guy, but I figured they weren't going to ask me to really kiss him, especially with my mom not around. Boy, was I wrong. When we were called into the cottage to audition, I played the scene the best I could without getting physical. The director stopped us. He excused the young man who was my acting partner, leaving just the director, the producer (another grown man), and me in the small back house.

"Look," the director said, "I will play the scene with you, okay? I want you to get this part, but you've got to do it right." He took me roughly by the arm and pulled me to him. "He holds you like this, okay?" I could feel his body against mine. It was hard and strange. I had a feeling he was enjoying the power he held over me.

"And you kiss him like this, okay?" He moved his head toward me. I moved my face away. "What's the matter, you don't want to do it?"

"No, no. I do. It's okay." I wanted to run like hell, but I had to be professional. What would my agent say? I couldn't piss the director off. I didn't dare.

We started the scene again. He was holding me so close I had to put my script to the side to look at the words. When it came time for the kissing part, I did the best I could. I held still, but I couldn't help flinching when he moved in for the kiss. I remember hearing the producer make a coughing noise that signaled this was getting awkward.

"Okay, okay, you're nervous," he said. "Do you not want this part?"

"I don't know. I think I should go. My mom is waiting for me in the car."

"Your mom is here? Where?"

"She's in the car outside. She said she was going to come in if I wasn't finished in a half hour. I should probably check in with her." I made that part up. It was a good lie in the moment.

Things suddenly changed in tone.

"Okay, well, you better go then. Go on!" His whole demeanor abruptly changed, and the energy in the room got really weird. I realized that if I hadn't had my mom waiting in the car, the situation could have progressed beyond what I would have been able to handle. I had no protection. No one was there to say, "Hey assholes, she's FIFTEEN. You could go to JAIL. Back off!"

That was not the first or last time something like that happened. I have lots of little stories about inappropriate hands, comments, words, and touches from very famous and not-so-famous men alike, who were far too attracted to young girls for their own good.

By the time I was twenty-two, I could barely tolerate being touched. I remember doing a play where I had an extreme reaction during rehearsal. In one scene, the actor I was working with suddenly grabbed me and pulled me to him. It was supposed to be a romantic gesture, but I felt totally invaded. My whole body went on alert, like some deep boundary in me had been crossed. I excused myself as politely as I could and went to the bathroom down the hall. Once inside, thinking no one could hear me, I began to kick the door of one of the stalls over and over. I was so angry I was being forced to allow a man to touch me again whenever and however he wanted. I realized I couldn't stand to be touched without my complete and total permission. I had no idea this was a normal reaction of trauma, stemming from years of abuse.

The director came into the bathroom. It turned out the noise of my kicking had echoed down the hall, back to the rehearsal room. I felt terrible. I told him that I had issues with being touched because of something that happened with my dad. I had never told anyone outside the family this. I couldn't go telling the whole cast that my dad had molested me, or that my mom had cancer and I was supporting everyone, or that the pressure was driving me over the edge. I was afraid it would come off as manipulative, or "victim-y." Not telling seemed to have the same effect. During the run of the play, one of the actresses (with her husband beside her, no less!) hissed at me and called me a cunt.

I know I was very lucky to have experiences of "movie magic" as a child. At the same time, I honestly and with all my heart beg parents NOT to put their kids in show business. No matter how great the film may be or how talented your kid is, there are things that can happen on a set that a parent cannot always control. It's an adult environment, not a playground.

Once youth is sacrificed to the movie gods, it cannot be returned.

The Wickedness
of the Scalene Triangle

❝Every man has inside himself a parasitic being who is act-
ing not at all to his advantage."
~William Burroughs

When I was ten, we moved to Newport Beach, twenty
minutes north of Laguna. My father said he thought he'd get
better clients in a richer community. (Looking back, I think
my income from commercials may have served to fund those
ambitions.) I didn't want to leave our quiet beach town. Life in
Newport was dominated by the idea of ownership. You either
"had" and were part of the acceptable clique, or you "had not"
and therefore were not. Back in Laguna, my friends were of
many variations—rich and poor, white and brown—I didn't
even know what social class was until we moved to Newport.
The girls at my school were mostly white and so well groomed
that it was hard to imagine they had any problems at all. I felt
like my burnished innocence let off a smell akin to burnt rubber, and as a result, I kept my distance.

The house we moved into was a three-story split-level

high up on a hill in a community called "Eastbluff." Behind our house a kumquat tree scattered fruit all over our backyard. Mom didn't like kumquats, so they just sat there and rotted. There was a strange "vibe" in that house—a feeling my mother attributed to her discovery that the land in Newport had once been Indian burial ground. She was pissed with the people who sold it to us for not revealing this fact. Indian bones there may have been, and smudging we may have needed, but she couldn't blame the Native Americans for what was about to happen in our family.

In order to begin a re-model that would ostensibly raise the value of the property, Mom ripped up all the carpets, pulled the wallpaper off, and knocked down a wall in the living room. Every room was like a mini construction site that smelled of mold, bleach, or plywood. We had to keep our shoes on to make sure we didn't step on a nail sticking out of the floor. During the two years we lived there, no room was completed. Dad was spending every dime both he and I made as soon as he could get his hands on it. He even bought himself a champagne-colored Cadillac—one of those hideous ones from the '80's with the trunk cut off. Little did our father's mistress know how corrupt a man he was, but she was about to find out. Oh boy, was she.

Yes, twenty years of nagging, crying, and fighting had left Dad with a desire to be nagged, tear jerked, and screamed at by someone younger, blonder, and thinner which, just like with our grandfather, took the clichéd form of his secretary.

It's funny to me how we can end up choosing partners like our parents, whether we want to or not. It seems we are almost magnetically drawn to the love we know from our childhood—

even if that love is incredibly flawed.

I once had a shrink tell me, "Listen, when you walk into a bar, find the man you are the most attracted to, walk over, then turn around and talk to the guy next to him."

If you can break the habit of being attracted to what you know, you've actually got a chance to not repeat your past. If your past is anything like mine, you've got all the motivation you need.

We found out about the secretary after my sister Annie spent an afternoon with her and our dad. The entire "father/daughter" outing had been secretly planned as a ploy to introduce her to his new girlfriend. When she got home, a disgruntled Annie immediately told Mom that during lunch Dad had said she should think of this complete stranger as her future step-mom. I remember clearly the look on Annie's face—it was as if this were all so ridiculous and stupid. Mom, however, was furious. Phone calls were made and suitcases were packed and flung onto the driveway.

When I heard that my parents were separating, not just fighting like they usually did, my disappointment was monumental. My dad wanted fancy cars and pretty girls and parties with important people—not bills and boogers and drunken fights and pregnant cats. He wanted to be a lover and a favored party guest seated next to the host, not a father kissing teddy bears and playing chess on the coffee table at home. I was deeply hurt and thought perhaps I had let him down by not allowing him to keep touching me that time.

Not long after he left, Sally, Mom's oldest friend, appeared at our house. She was roly-poly like our mom, with a similar sense of snappy humor, but much less cruel. She wore big glasses, had long hair, and (I suspected) smoked a fair amount of pot. I had no idea why we didn't see her more often, but guessed it was our mother who kept the distance. Mom did not like to be reminded of the past, nor did she like to tell her family or friends the truth about what was happening in her home. It was very unusual for her to allow Sally into this moment—her very public humiliation.

I remember sitting at the top of the uncarpeted split-level stairs, just outside my mother's paint-stripped bedroom door listening to her and Sally talk. As I listened for information about what exactly was going to happen now that Dad had left us, I contemplated the moving object in the laundry basket by the base of the stairs. It was a kitten. We owned three cats that had all gotten pregnant at the same time, and twenty-nine kittens were crawling out of their boxes all over the house causing a mewing hysteria. A mom-cat appeared and dragged the kitten out of the basket and hauled it *bump, bump, bump* down the second flight to the room below. She was keeping her babies together. I took this as a sign that I should go see what was happening in the grown-up bedroom.

Pushing open the door a crack with my foot, I could see Mom was sitting on her bed, head down. She had lost her battle with the past. I couldn't stand seeing her like that. Neither could Sally.

"You know, he did something weird when you were living in Los Angeles," began Sally, sitting on my parents' bed in her Birkenstocks and shorts. "He pushed me up against a wall and tried to kiss me. You were picking up one of the babies from daycare, I think. It was a long time ago, Dana. I'm really sorry I didn't tell you before, but you should know. He's not a good guy."

"Hey, that happened to me!" I piped in, poking my head in the half-open door. I just wanted to join the clan, to help my mother feel better, loved, and important. It felt like the right time to share. "He did that to me, too!"

The look on my mother's face was as if the air she had once breathed had turned to water. She was choking on it, going down wide-eyed and flailing. This was the opposite of the effect I wanted to have.

"He what?" She managed to barf up some air and a few spittle fish along with it.

"Well, I mean, it's just…what Sally said…I mean…that happened to me too. You know…with Dad."

Mom and Sally stared at me as I shifted back and forth on my sandaled feet, praying I wasn't going to be called a liar. I had the feeling I had made a terrible mistake—that I shouldn't have told the truth.

Earlier that year I had been hired as the national spokesperson for the "Strawberry Shortcake" dolls. Each doll was tiny and plastic and supposed to smell like a dessert. The whole group of them together gave off a sticky sweet smell, like an over ripe cantaloupe. We shot a series of four or five commercials all in one day. As I stood under the stage lights, I heard the clients whisper among themselves. My budding breasts were making tiny points under my pink, collared shirt. I was whisked away to a dressing room where a panicky wardrobe lady told me to wrap an ace bandage around my chest. I did as I was told. I didn't like it, but kept my mouth shut so I could keep my job. I learned then that not sharing my feelings was a key to survival. Why had I told Mom about that day with Dad? Instead of being welcomed into the tribe, I had made myself an outcast. I worried that maybe he wouldn't want to take me away anymore because I had told.

"Maybe it's hard to be a husband when your wife hates you so much," my twelve-year-old-self rationalized internally. "Maybe it wasn't his fault. Maybe he just wanted to be loved..."

Sally snapped me out of my childlike reasoning. "Dana, I think you need to file for divorce," she said gently to my mother. "I really think you have to."

First, Mom took me to a therapist.

Sitting on a leather chair in the office of what I was told was a "very nice lady who wants to listen to what happened between you and Dad" I thought about my family. I didn't want to hurt them. The lady across the room asked me questions, and I answered by giving truths wrapped in vagary. I told her I had a bad nap with Dad and it scared me. I had to take my glasses off because I started crying so hard the tears had made little pools inside the rims. The crying was supposed to give away the truth—it had been awful, terrifying. It had introduced me to a feeling in my underwear I never had before and wasn't ready to feel. Annie sat with me to be a witness. She handed me Kleenex one at a time as I cried, a concerned look on her round face. I felt so badly·for her—so guilty she had to listen to that story. She didn't seem shocked, just really sad for me.

When I couldn't think of anything more to say, Mom was called to take us out of the office. We sat in the car in the parking lot while Dad took his turn talking to the shrink. I hated the sense of responsibility and power I had over everyone—all over a moment that was so private. I hated causing them pain. I just wanted to go back to Laguna where my friends were, where dolphins leapt in groups headed toward Mexico. When Dad finally appeared outside the building, Mom got out to talk to him, leaving us in the car. Their bodies shimmered in the hard light of the noon sun as they stood in the parking lot. It was a brief conversation, after which she strode back to us, a truck of a woman hauling unknown burdens back to her two children.

She climbed into the driver's seat and started up the Mercedes with a roar.

"What happened? What did she say?" I asked. I wanted to ask, "Is Dad mad at me now?"

She was pissed. "She thinks you're lying. She talked to your dad and he won her over. He said he didn't remember doing anything. She thinks you must have made it up. Typical. Stupid bitch."

"What?" I asked, incredulous I had not made an impact. I was so shocked and ashamed I was shaking. "What did the lady say?"

"Nothing, Kate. She didn't believe you."

There was nothing more to say. In fact, not another word was spoken about that moment in our house. Ever. But something broke free in my mother after that, something primal and dangerous, and I discovered enough guilt and shame to last a lifetime.

Years later, I was sitting on a plane and the words going

around in my head sounded something like this:

*"My father abused and abandoned me. My mother humili-
ated and hurt me. What does that mean about me? If the people
I came from, who were supposed to love me the most, hurt me—
doesn't that mean I deserved it? Doesn't that mean I am a piece
of shit? Who am I if I'm not my father's child? Who am I if my
mother, who was supposed to love me beyond all, tortured me?
Who am I if a therapist, a professional who was supposed to be
able to decipher truth from fiction, did not believe my father molested me?" As I asked myself these questions as an adult, it left
me with a painful realization: I did not know who I was.*

After Dad moved in with his secretary, my parents put
the house up for sale and Mom, Annie, and I moved to a condo
at the bottom of "Eastbluff," near the "Back Bay" aka "swamp-
land." Apparently, Indians were smart enough to not bury their
relatives down there, so the "vibes" weren't as awful. I had
yet to learn that living in a condo in Newport was still doing a
hell of a lot better than 99.9% of the rest of the world, but as a
kid I didn't understand life in those terms. I only understood
intersections, the top and bottom of a hill, and the difference
between having a father and not.

The condo wasn't awful. It had nice white walls and short,
wall-to-wall gray carpeting. Mom bought new white sofas for
the living room and two blue foldout chairs for Annie and me to
crash on for the TV room. She gave much of our old furniture to
Dad. She didn't want too many reminders of the past.

Our days became very simple after that. Annie and I went
to school, came home, watched TV, and did homework. Mom
kept herself busy, too. When she wasn't talking to her law-

yer or driving me to an audition, she sewed, quilted, knitted, drank, baked, and tried to forget.

Jelly rolls, croissants, chocolate cakes, carrot cake with cream cheese frosting, muffins, scones, sour crème cheesecake with graham cracker crusts, "Grasshopper" ice cream cakes with ribbons of caramel and chocolate sauce on top, bread pudding with raisins, Angel food cake, Swedish pancakes with powdered sugar...sweet after sweet wafted daily through our afternoon kitchen. As they sat cooling on the counter, or chilling in the fridge, she continued to erase her memory with Scotch, bourbon, or vodka tonics.

There was an art to making Mom a drink, and I liked being good at it. I could caress the moment into a slow Kabuki-style dance of deference. It began with holding very still and waiting. If I did it right, it meant peace and quiet and maybe extra dessert later. When returning home from school, I would usually find my mother plopped in front of the TV. She would be sitting on one of the blue foldout chairs. Usually she'd be wearing a denim skirt with a stretchy waistband and a collared t-shirt, the preppy look of the 1980's.

"Kate, honey, come sit with me for a minute."

Her plump body took up most of the space on the chair, so I would sit by her feet and lean on her knees. Sometimes it would be a half-hour or more before I could move. While I waited for her next command, I would zone out on a detail outside—a tree limb that moved in the wind or a dog being walked on the community path beyond the low wall that separated our tiny garden from a manicured green hill.

"Be a darling and make me a drink, will you, sweetheart?"

Mom whispered.

And there it was, the permission. Permission to walk gracefully on my tip toes like a Japanese dancer into the kitchen. Permission to peer inside the beautifully organized cabinets for the bottle, to stand up tall like an adult and sort carefully through the good china to find the short round tumbler my mother liked best for Scotch with ice, her usual.

"How many ice cubes, Ma?"

I had to ask because it made a difference. Some days it was a full glass of cubes and Scotch three quarters to the top; other days it was only a couple of slim scalene triangles from the freezer and a half-inch of liquor.

"Oh, just a smidge. I gotta pick up your sister later."

I was happy to hear it. It meant she was only a little depressed, not the kind of mood that would last into the night and require all hands on deck. The ghosts in my mother's mind often refused her a single enjoyable moment, except during the first drink. Only then was there a short calm while the alcohol settled into her blood and the edge was cut. When the storm did come, as it often did, I could only hope it did not come my way.

One day I came home from a friend's house and found my mother sitting on the floor of her bedroom with a pair of scissors. The sliding, mirrored closet door was open. I could see ten or so of my father's neatly hung suits inside. They were Italian, bought at Neiman Marcus, Brooks Brothers, and Nordstorm's. Mom had been holding them hostage. Two more suits were sitting on the floor in a mound. A dark grey one and another—I think it was blue. He had spent thousands on these suits.

"Whatcha doin'?" I tried to sound nonchalant.

I watched my mother's eyes dart back and forth from me to the scissors to the buttons. She was carefully cutting each and every one off the jackets, then the pants of my father's suits.

"What does it look like, kid?" *Snip* went the scissors.

"I, um," I wiggled in my latest pair of white Bass sandals (I went through shoes quickly), trying to get the squeak out. "Why are you doing that?"

Mom's eyes suddenly popped up and stuck on me—red and sad, so sad. I was clearly interrupting. She put down her scissors, picked up her drink, and sighed—taking in my small but now threatening presence.

"Your dad wants his suits SENT to him, cocksucker piece of shit. Spends all your money on these suits, did you know that?"

I shook my head "No," but I didn't grasp the last part of what she said. I heard it—but it simply wouldn't enter my mind and lodge there to make sense.

Her drink and I sweated as she took another sip, the ice tinkling in the glass, her eyes waiting for me to say something. I think she wanted me to challenge her. Instead I said nothing and held very still.

She made a sour face at me and took a lady-like swig, pinkie out ever so slightly. I noticed she had recently painted her nails a pale peach, which I liked.

I didn't know what to say. "I'm gonna go watch TV, okay?"

I backed out of the room and hustled down toward the kitchen to make myself a peanut butter and jelly sandwich.

Mom didn't like it when I ate a big snack in the afternoon, but I figured she was too busy at the moment to notice.

"Whatever," I said to myself. "I need it." Peanut butter and jelly always made me feel more full and substantial. With my sandwich and fresh glass of milk balanced on a white Corcoran plate, I shuffled into the TV room and turned on the "boob tube." I could watch TV for six to eight hours in a row, sometimes more.

I clearly remember watching my first soap opera. I was four years old. That summer was hot, a dry heat cut only by the slap of water from a sprinkler. My babysitter, a lovely elderly woman named Fern, had a liking for The Young and the Restless. I remember because the announcer's voice stated it so distinctly, his baritone rich with intrigue and suggestion. Her son drove a bright green and orange truck full of Orange Crush. I could hear the glass bottles rattling in their refrigerated wooden boxes as he pulled in behind her house. I would almost always get to have one when I was there, fresh from the truck, all sticky sweet and cold. As I sat in front of the television, I floated in Fern's aura of certainty and gentleness like on a bubble of soda pop.

My twelve-year-old self needed to drown out what was happening upstairs, so I put my plate on the floor and turned on the soaps. The one that came on, *The Edge of Night*, was featuring an incredibly good-looking and charismatic actor with light brown hair and bright blue eyes. His blonde secretary was flirting with him, making him dance around his desk to avoid her overt, almost comical come-ons. I remember thinking I'd make a much better actress than her and shook my head. As she leaned over the businessman's desk, her breasts pushing the limits of her blue V-neck sweater, I stuffed in a big bite of peanut butter and jelly that had been soaking in my milk.

"Some things grown ups do make no sense," I said with my mouth full of peanut butter, to no one, or so I thought.

"What's wrong with you?"

I jumped. Holy cow. It was Mom. She could be so sneaky sometimes.

"Huh? What? Nothing!" I was worried she was going to yell at me for eating the sandwich. "What's wrong?"

She took a long look at me, then at the man on the television. "You know what, Kate? You have father issues." She announced. "I'm sorry he left, but you've got to get over it." She amazingly continued, "I think you need to go to a program for women who love alcoholics."

I looked at her like she had lost her mind. I didn't want to get a smack in the puss, and I didn't know how to say, "Why don't you go?" It would seem too raw, too tasteless somehow. But as my silence ate me, something ate my mother, and my mother ate. And drank. And drank. By late afternoon, she was bleary-eyed and sitting on my back picking my pre-pubescent zits.

"Get off! It hurts, get off!" Seeing Annie flash by my bedroom door, I screamed for her to help. "Annie...Annie!" I heard the sound of a door closing and a radio being turned on. She knew she was next.

"You can't go around with all these whiteheads on you! It's disgusting! Oh for God's sake, Kate, hold still, I'm almost done." My mother was holding a needle in her mouth for the big ones that wouldn't come out with picking.

"Stop, mom, please!" Tears poured down as the zits were popped and replaced by welts. A big bottle of hydrogen peroxide stood at the ready. I could tell one was infected if it made a sizzling sound when she put a peroxide-soaked cotton ball on it. This was an important lesson never to be forgotten. The sizzling.

"Hear how it makes that sound? Means it's infected. You gotta' keep putting the peroxide on until you don't hear that anymore."

File that one under "Important Motherly Wisdom."

After she was finished, we sat close together on the blue cotton sheets from Pick 'n Save that covered my twin bed. I blew my nose and investigated the needle and the damage done with my wet cotton ball as she sipped her Scotch, the hard triangular ice cubes now melted into the shape of little fish.

"You need to look out for that one," she said, pointing to the back of my arm. "See the white foam, the bubbles? Keep the peroxide on it. It will get better."

It was a strange and never forgotten form of affection. As we each took our turn, Annie and I would scream, weep hysterically, then wipe our eyes and apply the peroxide to our arms, back, and faces, wherever she had attacked, trying to take comfort in the idea that an infection was being purged. After we were cleansed of our evil, we'd climb inside our beds so we could feel the cool of the sheets against our raw skin.

At first I think my mother felt like a job had been well done. But perhaps the image of her two girls, sacked out with exhaustion from crying and screaming, began to wear on her, because that same day she decided to introduce us to a practice in which only adults should partake.

"There must be something I can do," I imagine she thought. "Something that will show them I'm just trying to help." And like Buddha under the Bodhi tree, she realized how to transform our pain into pleasure.

"C'mon girls! Downstairs!" Her voice sounded so light and happy it was unnerving. I lifted my head from the cool pillow and looked across my room toward her voice.

"Come down, it'll be fun! You'll love this, you sissies!"

We could hear her banging around the kitchen, which was usually a good sign. Maybe she'd make us brownies. I got up and went to the hallway that led to Annie's room and stuck my head in.

"You gonna go?" I could barely see Annie under her mound of covers. "Maybe she'll make us brownies and we can lick the bowl."

Annie lifted back the cover just enough so I could see her left cheek. It was red and swollen like she had been bitten by a hundred mosquitoes. I was suddenly grateful most of my zits were on my back and arms.

"You go. Tell me if it's brownies," she mumbled out from behind her braces. "I don't want to deal with anything else."

I wanted so much for it to be brownies that I raced downstairs with the decision to make sure it was, and if it wasn't, to achieve by all means necessary the requisite tone of begging needed to accomplish at least one small tray—at least for Annie because she was now looking like a mutilated pizza.

"Hey, Mom, are you making brownies? Will you make

brownies if you aren't yet making them already? Please?" I gave her my best "super cute" expression and at the same time made myself as small as possible, so she would see my total deference to her will.

"No, but I'm making something better," she said. "Get your sister down here."

I watched as she pulled out a giant silver Osterizer blender, the whole drawer of ice cubes, two cans of frozen lemon-limeade, and a big bottle of tequila.

Running to the bottom of the stairs, I yelled up, "ANNIE. MOM SAYS COME DOWN HERE NOW! SHE'S MAKING SOMETHING BETTER THAN BROWNIES!"

I knew I was taking the risk of getting Annie seriously pissed, but I desperately needed her to participate in the new mood. It would have been too depressing to let her lay up there alone. I think even Annie instinctively knew that to stay there meant calling up something too dark for her young mind to fade into, so she trudged down the stairs in her penguin head slippers—barely willing but present.

"Now watch carefully so you can make these yourself when I'm dead and gone." We stood close together—two mangled girls—and stared at our new mother. Happy Mommy.

"C'mon, help! Get out the big glasses with the stems—the green ones. Don't give me that look, Annie, learn something useful, smart ass!" Annie pursed her lips harder and got out the big glasses. She had come downstairs against her better judgment. There was nothing to do but go along, for now.

I had tasted alcohol before, but nothing like this. The cold, chopped up ice whirling around in the blender mixing with the cans of frozen concentrated lemon-lime aid looked cool and pretty, like a yellow winter wonderland. Our mom opened the top of the blender while it was still storming lemon-lime and handed me the bottle to pour in the tequila.

"Make sure to put in enough but not too much, or it won't bind to the juice. Look, can you see how the level has gone up about three or four inches? That's good, that's good, stop. STOP."

And it looked good. It looked cold and refreshing, and I wanted to press my whole back against it. After a minute or two, Mom turned off the Osterizer and set three thick, green translucent glasses in a row next to the blender.

As she poured the drink, she gave us our instructions. "Keep it simple: half a thing of ice, one can of lemon-limeade, then tequila. Keep the hat on the blender unless you're pouring in the booze, but do it slowly. You don't want it splashing out all over the place." The three glasses now stood at the ready like good little soldiers, filled with slowly melting yellow-green snow.

"Okay, girls. Don't say I never did anything for you. Drink up! Here's to your father dying a horrible, painful death!"

The frozen lemon-lime concentrate wrapped with ice and tequila molecules slid up sweetly into my mouth like a Coke Slurpie in the middle of a hot, dry summer.

"Mmmm! Brrr!" I said, doing a little chilly dance.

Then there was a second feeling, a new feeling—a smooth numbness. I started to get excited. It stopped the pain on my back! It felt like happiness! And the taste was different, too, like a new brand of sweet and spicy potato chip.

"Wow! This IS better than brownies, Mom!" I looked over at Annie, who was using a spoon that had cooled in her glass against her face. I wanted to make sure she was happy, too. "Yeah, Anns?"

"Hell, yeah," she said, nodding her head slightly, already buzzed on Sudafed. Allergies had followed her into teenage hell. "This is good shit."

Standing at the kitchen counter, glasses in hand, the three of us morphed into something other than mother and daughters—we were survivors. I could tell my mother liked this feeling of camaraderie.

"The first time I had these was with your father," she murmured, looking across the room toward where Mexico might be—and twenty years ago.

"Well," I said in a show of solidarity, "maybe we're better off without him."

"Here's to THAT," shouted Annie. I looked over and wondered what had gotten into her. Mom gave a knowing half smile and nodded her head. This was good. This was how things should be.

Then we were silent again.

I was twelve. My sister was fifteen. What the hell was our mother thinking?

Trying to extend the sudden relief from the strain that usually permeated our home, I shouted, "Hey, what's on TV tonight?"

Annie ghosted out of the room drink in hand, on the hunt for the TV Guide.

"What day is it?" she shouted from the other room.

I looked at the calendar on the wall. "Saturday!" I shouted back.

"*Love Boat! Fantasy Island!* Whoo Hoo!" Annie whooped, staying where she was and flipping on the TV.

"Hooray! Hey, Mom, can we have Mexican food? Will you make brownies?" It was a good night to push it.

That's how margaritas and TV on Saturday night, and sometimes other nights, too, became our ritual for the next few years. It was a way to not worry about the future. Not to think about the past. Not to be afraid of the monster mother and for the mother monster to not worry about money.

Money. Money to pay for the house, food, clothes, insurance; money to pay for the car, the gas, the electric bill, the tap classes, donuts, and movie nights; money that held together a small army of three abandoned women and preserved some tiny sliver of the dignity one man had so casually walked out of the house with on just another sunny California day.

The Memory Thief

I had continued to take tap classes since the Guinness
event, and by the age of twelve was studying twice a week
at The Danny Daniels' School of Tap in Santa Monica. Mr.
Daniels was set to choreograph the film, *Pennies From Heaven*,
a musical starring Bernadette Peters and Steve Martin. The
story was about two poverty-stricken lovers who survive the
1929 Depression by fantasizing they are rich and glamorous.
After a challenging audition at the dance school, I was chosen to play one of the children inside a moldy city schoolroom
where Ms. Peters' character was teaching. Children who, in
her daydream, would morph into beautiful dancers dressed all
in white, tap dancing and jumping up and down off tiny white
pianos as a newly fashioned Ms. Peters sang, *"Love is good for
anything that ails you, baby, there ain't nothin' love can't do…"*

Five days a week for an entire month, Mom and I would
drive up to MGM studios at 4 a.m. so I could rehearse with Mr.
Daniels and eventually, Ms. Peters. Every day the children
would learn and practice the various routines that were to be
shot the final week of that month. When we weren't rehearsing,

we had costume fittings, makeup tests, and school.

I enjoyed drifting in and out of the magical world the production was creating. One morning, as we were walking across the studio back lot to the sound stage that was our combined school and waiting area, I noticed there were hundreds of plastic golden "pennies" all over the street. The night before had been spent shooting a scene where they had fallen from the sky as a man danced and sang, "Every time it rains, it rains, pennies from heaven." I ran and scooped up as many as I could, stuffing them into my pockets. I knew they had no value, but they made me feel very rich.

When we finally started shooting the dance sequence, it was like being inside one of those Easter eggs that has a hole inside where you peek in to see the tiny rabbits or chicks dressed in top hats. This time, however, I was on the inside, in a pretty white dress made of satin and tulle, surrounded by sparkling white floors and walls, tiny white pianos and instruments, and silver glitter. As I looked out toward the camera, I could see the dank walls of the soundstage, the greasy mechanisms of the camera tracks, and the pale, grizzled face of the director, Herbert Ross. Motivated by his fierce expression, I danced better than I had in my life, losing myself in that Depression-era child and making her fantasies my own.

It was around this same time as the film shoot that I began to drift in my mind to imagine in greater detail what other people's lives were like. I started to watch people to see if they were talking, if they were happy, and sometimes, what they were wearing.

Back in our neighborhood, we picked up some burgers

to go. As we drove, I gazed at the houses going by, wondering what was happening inside them—if they were a family of four and if they felt "normal" and loved by one another. I imagined being the girl who worked at the counter inside the Jack in the Box restaurant, envisioning the details: What kind of jeans did she wear? What were her parents like? Probably roly-poly and kind, proud that she had a job. I bet she had her own car, too, maybe even a boyfriend. It seemed like a nice life. I thought about it so fervently that suddenly for a moment I was the girl at the counter—leaning out of the fast food pick up window, happy to pass warm burgers to the hungry citizens of the County of Orange. I brushed back what was now my black hair in the reflection of the window and slipped on some shiny pink lip-gloss, tossing a joke to the manager. This scene made me laugh out loud.

"What's so funny?"

Oops. Mom was staring at me.

"Kate, I swear to god, if you are making fun of your mother, I'm going to slap the crap out of you."

"No, no! I was just thinking about the girl in the Jack in the Box."

"Oh. Yeah. What a slut."

As we pulled out into traffic, I immediately erased all dreams about becoming a Jack in the Box worker and tried to focus on the burger she had just handed me. I was glad there was a pickle on it and wondered if the worker had snuck it on there especially for me, somehow sensing my fondness for pickles.

When we got home from the restaurant, Mom had fallen

into a foul mood. A gift had arrived from my father—a small wooden statue from Jakarta—and she didn't like it. I watched as she went into the garage and returned with a small hand axe. She then placed some newspapers on the floor in our front hallway and proceeded to methodically chop the statue with the axe. She was very neat. As she chopped, I started to imagine myself chopping, too. I could feel her anger as it passed into me and took a small hold.

Suddenly, I had a funny feeling I was going to miss out on some things—some "growing up type things" I couldn't quite put my finger on. I promised myself I would make them up later. This moment required sacrifice. This moment required the axe.

Gratitude

It is simply impossible to go on with this story without cataloging a few things I am forever grateful to my parents for. 1) Dying young. (Now Cady, that's awful, you don't mean that.) 2) Teaching me how <u>not</u> to drink. (Not 100% sure I learned that one.) 3) Spending all the money I made as a child so I would learn how to be a hard worker as an adult. (This still boggles my mind.) 4) Showing me how <u>not</u> to treat your lovers, neighbors, friends, or colleagues. (Okay, now I am sounding bitter, time to stop screwing around.)

I am getting off track here. It is important for you to know before I tell you about the worst of it (yes, it gets worse), that I know my mother was gifted, tried hard, and was loving in her way. She was a very good cook, a creative and stylish house maker, and a devoted student of art—both the history and the practice. She wrote poetry and short stories and collected a vast array of musical instruments, all of which I was allowed to play. She believed in the pleasures of the artistic life, and by example showed me that it is possible and perfectly acceptable to practice as many arts as one might feel called to explore.

Mom also liked to go to museums. I saw all the major museums of Los Angeles by the time I was fifteen, including the J. Paul Getty, The Los Angeles Museum of Art, and of course the wonderful Natural History Museum with the La Brea Tar Pits. Hopefully, all kids in L.A. get a school tour of the Pits. Evolution is no joke, and the bones of the dinosaurs are a good example for kids to learn how nature is always up to her funny tricks. It may be disturbing for a kid to see the fake baby Mammoth trapped in the tar, but it is also a profound lesson in the importance of staying close to the group.

My mother also regularly took my sister and me to all three of The Los Angeles Music Center's theaters: The Ahmanson, The Mark Taper Forum, and The Dorothy Chandler Pavilion. We saw Frank Langella in *Dracula,* Bob Fosse's production of *Dancin',* and all thirteen brilliant hours of the Royal Shakespeare Company's *Nicholas Nickleby* (with the original London cast). It was so good we saw it twice. We saw *Evita* with Patty LaPone and Mandy Patinkin, *Burn This* with John Malkovich, and *Sweeney Todd* with Angela Lansbury and George Hearn— all before I was fifteen years old. It was an incredible art and theatre education, for which I have our mother solely to thank. I don't recall our father attending a single production.

Dad did give me one good experience that I can recall. He took me on the back of his motor scooter for a drive around our Laguna neighborhood when I was seven. Despite the fact I was barefoot, I had a feeling of absolute safety. Trees flashed by us, the pavement becoming a blur under my soft toes. It felt so good to ride through the twilight with the wind blowing my hair, free from worry and fear.

My father also liked swimming in the ocean, which I did not. The waves were too big, and I always got caught in them and sucked down to the ocean floor. But he would go past where the waves broke to swim with the seals. I watched their heads bobbing up and down from the safety of the beach. I'm still not much of a swimmer, but when I am out in nature, I feel the better part of him close to me, and for that I am grateful.

Homecoming

One day after driving around for hours with my mother, we returned home to our condo to find a large brown Labrador retriever sitting inside the gate that separated our front patio from the sidewalk. The dog's eyes looked tired, and her stomach hung down over her feet.

"It's Dinah! Mom, Dinah!"

Dinah was our family dog. She had been living with Dad since the separation. Mom had decided that if our father was going to live with his secretary, the least he could do was take the dog off her hands and leave her one less mouth to feed. My sister and I missed her, even though we loathed the chore of walking her and picking up her enormous mounds of chocolate-colored poop.

As we pulled into the driveway, Dinah's ears perked up and her head swung in the direction of our car. I grabbed onto the seatbelt buckle so I could snap it open as soon as we stopped. The dog being back was a sign that our home life might be turning toward the positive.

Back when we lived in Laguna, I once saw Dad holding

Dinah up by the scruff of her neck, at least two feet off the ground, while hitting her hard with the palm of his hand. The sound of the dog's terrified screams shot through me. I wanted to wrap Dinah up in blankets of kindness after that—to make her forget that anyone had ever hurt her so badly for some mild, dog-like offense.

As Mom turned off the car, her shook her head.

"God dammit," she muttered as she knelt down in her tweed slacks, her knees cracking, "Look at her. That bastard." She reached down and felt the dog's belly. "She's pregnant."

Dinah took a big sigh and lay down as I wrapped my arms around her.

"It's okay," I whispered in her soft ear, "We'll take care of you."

Suddenly Dinah started whining and pooping puppies all over. She even pooped one out in the driveway. Mom started screaming and laughing at the same time, "Oh my God! Find the puppies, girls! Find the puppies!"

Annie and I ran all over, searching for puppies in the bushes like we were hunting for Easter eggs, shouting, "Got one!" every time a pup was found. We put them in a big plastic hamper, dizzy and vaguely nauseous from the strangely sweet smell of shit and doggie afterbirth. Although I felt bad for Dinah's agony, I couldn't deny the joy I felt over the new life pulsing out of her in wet gelatinous globs.

Finally we managed to usher our dog's waddling, exhausted body into an impromptu space in the garage by the washer/dryer to poop out the rest—ten huge black and brown puppies in all. She didn't have the teats to feed so many, so Mom bought baby bottles and spent the afternoons while we were at school helping Dinah feed her puppies. She wrapped each fragile pup in a fresh blanket, holding it close to her breasts while it nursed from a bottle. Watching her be so gentle, I wished we had more baby animals, not less, but in time all the puppies were given away.

Meanwhile, my mom had tracked down our father and given him an earful about the dog. Since he was a rancher's child, his sense of humor and method of communication apparently had a lot to do with raw surprises. He told us once that the best way to take revenge against someone was to put a pile of dog shit in a paper bag, douse it with kerosene, put it on the front step of his or her house, light it on fire, ring the doorbell, and run. The first instinct of the person who answers the door will be to stomp on the bag of fire, in so doing covering his or her foot in crap.

Apparently, my dad thought a pregnant dog would be a funny way to reach out.

"Just my way of saying hi," he mumbled into his end of the phone. The secretary and he were having problems. He was having second thoughts about the divorce.

After they talked for a while, Mom hung up the phone and made a surprising announcement. "Your father...Ahem!" she coughed, looking like a child who had been caught making a terrible mistake. "Your father is coming home for a while."

We froze.

"Well?" She looked at us as if we were supposed to leap up in the air and celebrate this amazing news. "Say something, girls!"

Although it was against everything we had been committed to, at this point I was willing to act however she wanted, as long as it meant a conflict-free moment. Frankly, I would have danced naked on the roof if it meant a days worth of peace and calm in the house.

"Wow! Okay! Great!" I threw out any positive words that came to mind, all the while watching my sister from the corner of my eye. "Right, Anns? Whoo Hoo!" I could tell Annie was trying with every ounce of effort she had not to say something that came off as sarcastic.

"Thrilling," was all she could manage. "I can't wait." She quickly blew her nose. "I think I'm having allergies again. Do we have any Sudafed?" I think her plan was to just pop them all day until he left again.

It was incredibly bizarre to see Dad living in our condo after all everything that had happened. Despite all, there he was—sitting on the sofa, drinking a beer, and digging in the cupboards for chips. Annie and I were nervous that Mom might turn on us for having once been against him, even though we did it for her, so we stayed very quiet. It was better to be quiet when things were strangely normal, and our father seemed to be making an actual effort.

Looking back, it's amazing to me how the slightest promise of stability was able to override so much of the past for us: his long absences; the cruel insults and twisted jokes he threw at us whenever he was in a bad mood; wondering where his hand was going to fall in a drunken hug...those unforgotten insults could all be gently put aside for the promise of something that smelled like normalcy. It was as if he subconsciously knew that the love of his family was the only way for him to access any sense of dignity or self-respect. Like some kind of primal response—our love alone allowed him the illusion that there was some substance to his flailing and insecure character. When our love faltered, even by the tiniest bit, his monstrous ego had to run elsewhere to be fed.

"Normalcy" lasted about three weeks until like every time before, "Bill McClain: The Broken Record" was gone. Mom, Annie, and I went back to our routine of margaritas and TV and school like nothing had ever happened.

About a week later, I came home after another normal day at school where nothing terribly interesting happened except my teacher had yelled at me about using black lines around my drawings. She had specifically told us not to, but I had always put black lines around my drawings. Otherwise how would the colors know where they were supposed to be? Irritated, I stomped into the condo and found Mom standing in the kitchen with her drink, holding several pieces of light purple paper in her hand. There were no black lines on it. It was all purple—purple paper, purple writing—which I knew, even if my teacher didn't, meant trouble.

Mom looked strangely triumphant.

"Well girls, the SLUT is back. And she wrote YOU. Would you like to hear what she has to say?"

We didn't know whether to be honest but knew when in doubt not to be. In an unusual move, Annie stepped up to the conversation. "Sure, Ma. What did she say?"

I stood frozen.

"She wants to be your FRIEND, and I, apparently, your

MOTHER, I am an emotionally disturbed MONSTER, HA!"
She took a swig from the tumbler. "She wants you to know that
she is IN LOVE with your father and wants to be your friend,
YOUR FRIEND! Give me a goddamn break. Look! Look for
yourselves." She pushed the paper in Annie's face.

Annie took it like a piece of homework with a bad grade
and sniffed it. I got up and looked too, honestly curious about
the woman who was taking our father away from us again, as
well as the strange smell emanating from the purple paper.

I noticed the woman's handwriting was round and playful,
like that of a high school student. I had to admit that even I, at
the age of twelve, would not write a letter with a purple pen.
I thought either the pen was candy scented or the paper had
been sprayed with some kind of "teen beat" perfume, as if she
had perhaps been trying to relate to kids our age. There was
even a little heart over one of the "i's". I wanted a chance to
meet this woman on my own terms and make up my mind, but
Mom hated her so much I doubted there would be that chance.

"So. She wants to meet you and be your FRIEND. Do you
want to meet her, girls? BE HER FRIEND?" Mom suddenly
looked like one of those bears in the Alaska wilderness, huge
and hungry, and not huggable. Annie got up and looked in the
fridge, a technique she had recently invented to diffuse the sensation of stress rising up in her stomach—a dangerous move in
the middle of one of our mother's dramas. I was impressed.

Then Annie spoke again. "You know what, Mom? I don't
care." She tried looking casual as she pulled a can of Diet Coke
free from the plastic rings that held five other cans captive.
"But really, do I have a choice?"

As she popped open the can and turned away to get a glass for ice, I decided my sister was the bravest person I had ever met.

Mom stood quietly for a moment. Her opera interrupted. I could see her trying to decide whether to smack Annie in the puss or not. The Diet Coke started to bubble up in the glass.

I decided to throw in with my sister, as if this ritual behavior might trigger a return to calm. "Can I have one, Anns?"

It was just a Diet Coke, not a statement of loyalty for our father's girlfriend. It was our way of saying, "Please, Mom, enough with the emotional drama. We are just kids. Enough," but you would have thought we were packing our bags for Egypt and giving our mom the finger while smearing dog shit on the walls. Her face was covered with an expression of total betrayal. Her eyes began to well up.

"Okay. I see what's happening. Go ahead, you two. Gang up against your mother. Why don't you go stay with The Slut and your father for a while? Go ahead. En-joy." She picked up her glass of Scotch and started to head up the stairs. "You'll appreciate me then, that's for sure. Good fucking luck."

We heard her bedroom door slam shut.

I stared at Annie and my thoughts started flying. "What just happened? Were we going to have to go live with our father? Was this a possible good thing? No. No, it couldn't be. Not with OUR father and certainly not with some strange woman we didn't even know. I started to get really anxious and Annie felt it.

"C'mon Kate, let's watch TV." She headed into the living room. "Drink your Coke, okay?" I took the glass with ice and looked up toward the stairs. A shit storm was coming and I didn't like the feeling. Somebody was gonna get it.

I decided to go up.

"I'll be right back, okay?" I piped, hoping it would sound assuring.

"I wouldn't if I were you." Annie was no fool. She knew what I was thinking.

"It's okay. I'll be right back."

I had to go. I had to prostrate myself at my mother's feet or who knew what would happen later.

I tiptoed as quietly as I could up the stairs—the only sound I made the ice in my glass. The scalene triangles moved around gently, like frozen fish bumping against each other with big frozen eyes. They stared up and silently asked me, "Are you sure about this?"

I wasn't. I stopped and listened at Mom's door for a sound that would translate what was going on inside and if it was safe to interrupt. There was nothing.

I took a breath and turned the door handle slowly.

"Mom? Are you okay?" I knew she was far from okay, but it was best to be polite. "Can I come in?"

"Kate...what is it, honey?" She was lying on the bed, looking out the window.

I made my silent Kabuki moves toward the bed and quickly lay down next to her, wrapping my arms as best as I could around her mountainous frame.

"I just wanted to make sure you were okay." I held my breath and tried to guess where she was looking, as if that could give me a sign of her thoughts.

"I'm fine. I'm just tired. You go on downstairs and watch TV with your sister. I'm gonna nap for awhile." This put me on the alert. It was the "be with your sister" part that sounded wrong. There would be shit tonight without a doubt.

"We love you, Mom!" I cried out, "We don't want to live with The Slut!"

Suddenly, I noticed another presence in the room. Annie. She felt the storm coming too and had decided to rise above her drama exhaustion to make an effort. Mom rolled over and looked at us both.

"I can't deal with you guys ganging up on me, okay? It's not fair." Tears started rolling down her face, and Annie rushed over to her other side. We threw our arms around her and hugged her hard.

"We love you, Mom! We love you! Fuck The Slut! Fuck Dad! They are assholes, okay? We love YOU!" We hoped by swearing it would emphasize how much we meant what we said, but it didn't seem to get a rise out of her at all.

Annie and I looked at each other once or twice as her sobbing continued, and when that felt weird, looked at the wall, a chipped corner on the chest of drawers, or a piece of thread coming out of Mom's pants. We knew we just had to ride this out because a cry like this only happened when things were really bad. The only way to handle it was to suck it up and comfort her, make her a drink, take the Lean Cuisines out of the freezer for dinner, and calm her down. Once she got a drink in her, we'd make her another one, pop the Lean Cuisines in the microwave, and turn on the TV. Divide, distract, and conquer. That night, as if she knew our routine for pulling her out of a funk, she pulled a unique move.

"It's okay, girls. I'm okay now, really. Thank you. Go watch TV now, okay? I'm gonna rest for a while."

She closed her eyes as if she was going to nap. Annie and I stood over her, wondering if a nap was really going to make a difference, but we had no choice. There was no arguing with her now. We had to submit to her will.

Annie said nervously, "I've got a lot of homework." She picked up her watery Diet Coke, carefully wiped the condensation from the glass off the dresser with her sleeve, and walked out of the room.

This was my sister's cue that she needed to be left alone but I didn't want to be alone. I was a kid and needed my childhood playmate to make everything okay again. I decided what Annie really needed was distracting, not studying, and whispered through a crack in her bedroom door where it didn't close all the way.

"Wanna play cards for a while?" There was no answer, so I tried again. "Wanna play a game?"

When we were little, we had made up wonderful games. One of them was "Secret Friend." In the game, Annie would leave notes for me in her room to discover. The notes were special missives from the planet Jupiter where my secret friend "Miranda" lived. Her missives contained notes about the weather in space or if "Miranda" had a cold or taken a trip. The letters would be found on Annie's desk, which of course, Annie couldn't "see" because they had special Jupiter dust on them. Only "Miranda" and I could. Sometimes the letters would warn of "Miranda's" imminent arrival. This would be a very special occasion. We would have to do it when the parents weren't looking because no one could know I had a friend on another planet.

I loved this game.

"Miranda? Are you in there?" I got hopeful. I knew Annie liked this game, too.

Annie's irritated voice boomed from behind the white plywood door, "PLEASE, KATE, LEAVE ME ALONE."

"Just, uh, haven't heard from Miranda in a while. Wondered what she was doing." I thought it didn't hurt to ask.

There was silence for a moment.

"I THINK SHE'S DOING HER HOMEWORK, TOO."

Mom woke up around dinnertime and took the Lean Cuisine's out of the freezer. She looked more exhausted than before the nap. We ate quietly in front of the TV, going straight to bed after the *Million Dollar Movie*.

That night I dreamt I was in the film *The Outsiders* with the actor C. Thomas Howell. I had developed quite a crush on C. Thomas, even cutting out his picture from the newspaper and pinning it on my bedroom wall. In the dream, Johnny was telling Pony Boy to "Stay gold." Somehow, I was Pony Boy, which confused me. I was supposed to be Cherry Valance—the pretty girl they all liked—my hair flying free in the cold night air. I was trying to force my dream into behaving when I heard a voice too loud to be in my head.

"C'mon Pony. Pony, wake up."

I didn't want to wake up. I wanted to be Cherry Valance. I certainly didn't want to try and understand the words coming out of my mother's mouth.

"Kate, wake up. Listen to me. I'm leaving."

I sat up, dizzy from the intensity of the dream. "What? Where are you going?"

Mom was sitting on my bed. "I'm going to kill your father and his girlfriend. I'm telling you now so that if I don't come back, you'll know what happened."

I knew my mother owned a gun. I had seen it, and so had Annie. It sat in a dingy cardboard box next to her side of the bed. I had opened it and looked one time. It was solid black iron, with a brown wooden handle. It now sat in my mother's shaking hand.

"What?" I sat up and watched her walk like a ghost out of my bedroom down the stairs to the garage below. "What?"

The air around me began to break apart like pieces of a puzzle.

I got up and woke up Annie.

"Annie, wake up. Mom says she gonna kill Dad or herself," was all I could get out. I don't know why I thought to add she was going to kill herself. I can't remember whether she had said that or not, but it felt like a possibility, so I had to say it was. The next thing that happened is a blur, but I remember us both running downstairs in our Lanz nightgowns, screaming at the top of our lungs—high, shrieking, gut-wrenching wails, hoping she would hear us and stop. We lost all control. Instead of going into the garage, we sat holding each other's hands on the new white sofa in the living room. We didn't dare follow her. She had a gun. When we heard the car start, we went even wilder, so she could hear us over the engine. We wanted to wake the neighbors, God, somebody, anybody.

Finally, we heard the car turn off. She came inside. She wasn't holding the gun anymore.

"Go to bed, girls. I'm not going do it. Go to bed now."

We wouldn't move.

"BED. NOW. MOVE."

We did as we were told, knowing it had cost us everything—that we had broken ourselves in two and there would be no piecing the broken parts back together, ever.

There would be no more dreaming about Pony Boy, either.

As our mother continued to disintegrate, the house began to feel like it was booby-trapped. No matter where we stepped safely yesterday, it could have been rewired for combustion today. Annie started breaking out in hives, popping Sudafed, and refusing to leave her room. I tried to keep busy in my room drawing pictures. I did a whole series featuring Annie and me as lambs. In some drawings we fought crocodiles. In others we were flying away to South America on a giant bird.

After our mother's episode with the gun, I missed my sister terribly, even though she was right in the next room. It just wasn't safe for us to talk much anymore.

The Beating

❝C'mon Kate, wanna go for a drive?" Mom was in a chipper mood. Drive time was usually a good sign that things were safe for the moment. Feeling like I shouldn't leave her alone, I had begun to ride with her in the car whenever she would go on errands. I'd fiddle with the radio or put my feet out the window to feel the breeze when she wasn't tense. Driving together like this became a shared moving meditation. It didn't really matter where we went as long as we were driving, moving—the air flowing over and past us—the people outside the car and us within. It was the most relaxed my mother would be, the only time she might hang her arm out the window or put on her sunglasses to look cool.

"Your father called and wants to talk again. I thought I'd go see him at the office, wanna come?"

I held out hope that this all was just a bad moment in time. I missed my dad and the comparable stability he brought with him—unlike Annie and I, at least he was allowed to fight back. Plus, he had no idea that we had recently saved his life, and I thought maybe he should know.

"Be right down!" I stopped by Annie's closed door for a moment, "We're gonna go see Dad. Wanna come?" I thought it was right to ask; he was her father, too. A part of me hoped Annie would suddenly become the adult in the whole situation and throw a fit about the madness.

Instead, I heard a deep sigh.

"You're funny." I could see my sister in my mind's eye looking up from her papers and her Kleenex, shaking her head at my folly. "Homework."

The door stayed shut.

It was a beautiful afternoon for a drive. The sky was a bright, blinding blue. A breeze brushed across the trees and flowers like an invisible goddess caressing her favorite children. I dreamily watched the sun reflect off the windows of the car into star-shaped patterns. Mom always kept the car so it smelled like Armor All and Windex. Clean and sharp. I opened up the glove compartment and took out a container of Nosecoat, a sunblock that my dad used when he went running. I had found it in the bathroom before he left and asked if I could keep it because I liked the smell. It smelled like summer.

As we neared Dad's office, I noticed the glass-covered buildings gleaming—the trees and sky reflected back to all who approached. Mom pulled the Mercedes into a parking space by the front door. The building mirrored back to us how small we were compared to the wealth and beauty around us.

"Hang here, Kate, I'm just gonna run in."

She had put her nice skirt on, shimmied into stockings and applied lipstick. Perhaps the three of us were going to go to a restaurant. I knew the gun had been left behind in her bedside drawer—I made sure to look before we left. There would be no blood bath today, not if I could help it. I glanced around from my co-captain's position in the front seat and decided that being an adult looked terrible. Day after day of sitting inside air-conditioning while the sun warmed the whole world to relaxed perfection outside. I decided then that there was no way I would work in an office when I grew up. I'd rather blow my brains out.

Mom appeared looking hurt.

"He's not there. They said he went out with his secretary. Put your seatbelt on."

I had taken mine off so I could scoot down in the seat and hang my feet out the window while I waited. I barely had time to click the belt into place before we tore out of the parking lot.

"What's going on?" I asked, stuffing my feet back into my sandals. I didn't like being in the front seat when Mom drove like her hair was on fire. "Where are we going?"

"We're just going to have a little look. Gonna see if we can find them. Look around, Kate. Look for your bastard father." I noticed her hands were shaking again.

I didn't want to look anymore. I just wanted to stop the car, make my mother get out, and drive us both home myself. I certainly didn't want to see what I did—Dad and some petite blonde woman in a blue skirt suit, holding hands and walking down the sidewalk on their way back from somewhere nearby—presumably lunch.

"Mom…" I pointed at them with my eyes, and then she saw them, too. I could feel the image of them together hitting her like a thousand knives all at once. I felt so bad.

I wished to God that I had never said anything. I wished that I were older. I wished I were a stone. I closed my eyes and wished more than anything that I was back with Annie, watching TV and drinking margaritas.

Mom pulled the car over, slamming on the brakes—not too violently but enough to shake me up and out of my disappearing act. I had to watch her turn off the car and get out. I had to hear my mother's voice shaking as she spoke to my dad and the woman who used purple pens that smelled like candy.

Out of nowhere, my mother started hitting the blonde in the blue suit. Hitting her hard in the face. Blood exploded from the woman's head—spilling down her left cheek and onto her pretty light blue blouse. She looked horrified and held up her hands to stop the beating. Mom just stood there like a massive tree trunk and hit, spurting this poor woman's blood into the blue sky in showers.

Dad looked on, frozen in time. Bill McClain: the man, the myth, the father—just stood there and did nothing. I heard the woman say, "Help me, Bill," but he didn't move.

Then Mom stopped, just for a second. It was enough time for the other woman to realize that Bill wasn't going to do anything, so she had to run if she didn't want to be killed. She ran right down the middle of the street, tripping on the goddess of perfection's beautifully paved asphalt. We stood there and watched her fall. There must have been a rock, one tiny pebble that the goddess had misplaced that had found its way beneath the heel or toe of this woman's little blue pump. It sent her reeling forward in slow motion, arms flailing, grasping at the air as if it would steady her. Her knee hit first, ripping her stockings open, and underneath, her skin, followed by her hips, hands, and chin. I knew how much that hurt. I had done that plenty of times falling off my bike or my skates. Her hands would need hydrogen peroxide and lots of it. She would have to listen for the sizzling now.

As her tiny body disappeared down the white-lined asphalt, I noticed something moving out of the corner of my eye and turned my head to look. There was another family standing there, just across the street—a mother, a father, two girls, and a photographer, who had been composing a family portrait against some delicate flower plantings. They, too, had seen everything and done nothing.

Nobody was moving.

Then I heard a strange sound coming out of Mom. A moan.

"Ohhhh...God. Take me home, Bill. Please, take me home." She was looking at her blood-covered hands.

I wished so much I could run out and stand in the picture of the family across the street, to go home with them to a normal dinner and a normal night of TV and squabbling and doing homework. As I looked at their faces, something else sank in that moment. Like a ship going down that would never come up again, I knew I would never get a chance to become something other than what my mother needed me to be—not unless I ran away or somebody dropped dead. I had to pay attention, to play my part and be the audience my parents needed me to be—or at the very least the clear thinker in case things got worse.

I got out of the car and stepped toward my parents.

"Dad, can you drive us home? Please?"

My father was finally starting to move his face. He was angry. He couldn't even look at me. Instead he stared at his soon-to-be ex-wife—his weak hate growing on itself.

"Please, Bill, please! I'm upset! Just drive us home!"

That's when I noticed my mother's keys. They were covered in blood. She had forgotten she had her key ring in her hand and had hit the woman in the face while holding her giant metal ring of keys. This accounted for the blood bath.

My father muttered, "No. No. Damn it. No."

I watched him stand there in his beautiful Brooks Brothers suit—the suit that he would rather buy and dry clean and have the buttons sewn back onto than give the money to his wife to feed their children. He had a dumbfounded expression on his face—mouth open, eyes focusing and un-focusing, trying to take in what had just happened. I took a picture of him in my mind just in case I never saw him again. He was so beautiful, so slim, so tan, and such a coward. Why did he have to be such a coward? I wanted to tell him about the gun. I had to tell him that this was not as bad as it could have been...but no more words would come out of me.

As my mother stood defeated and un-chosen, I had a deep pang of compassion for her. It was awful to see her so humiliated. Of course she hit back. It was almost natural, almost right. A woman did not give everything to a man, bear his children, make his home, and guide his life to have her love replaced by someone who didn't earn it—whose only obvious qualities were her youth and her slim figure. It was the lowest blow I could think of, this exposure to our replaceability my father had allowed by being too cowardly to do anything but serve himself. I wished so badly I could drive. My God, I wished I could drive. I wanted to put my mom in the backseat and take her to a hospital or to somebody who knew about these things so she could be stopped. Someone had to stop this insanity that had taken over our lives so completely.

My father took one last withering look at his wife—fat and shaking and covered with blood and tears. Without looking at me, he turned and walked as quickly as he could to where the small blonde woman had run. I watched the sun reflect off his polished black shoes—my father's shoes—moving swiftly down the California sidewalk glinting with bits of mica. He didn't look back.

There was no computing this situation for me at the time. It just fell into a sort of void; the place where events that one cannot reason go. He had to leave, that was all.

I turned back to my mother who was slowly, almost gracefully reaching down into herself and picking up some piece of her pride that had fallen—pride put back into grasp now that the blonde had been beaten down. She was a warrior. She had an axe and a gun and a ring of keys. I watched her wipe her shaking, bloody hands on her skirt as she took a deep breath.

"In the car, Kate."

Her physical presence had unexpectedly now taken on something regal. She stopped being hysterical and became very calm. Not knowing what else to do, I got back in the car and put my seatbelt back on. I felt so tiny next to my mother, as if I could float out into the sky.

"Whatever happens next...happens next," was all I could think. "Be practical. Be the voice of practicality here."

"You okay to drive?" I had to ask.

"Yes. I think we should go home. We will go home and wait for the police to call."

"The police?" The word sounded foreign, as it was supposed to.

"Yes." She started the monster Mercedes with a roar and put it in gear.

I blinked my eyes and looked out the window to where the other family had been standing and had since disappeared. "Okay, Ma."

I wondered where the other family went and if I would get to go live with them now, or if the police would send me to an orphanage. I worried about what would happen to Annie and if we would stay together. Then I realized I'd have to tell her what had just happened.

Poor Annie. She just wanted to be left alone to do her homework. I knew I was bringing home something bad, and I felt really guilty. It sucked to be the bearer of bad news, but Annie couldn't hear this from our mother. Oh no. It had to be from me. I'd have to get upstairs before Mom and hide the gun, too.

As we pulled up to the condo and parked, I ran into the house. I needed the safety of Annie, even if for just a minute, but Mom was right behind me.

"I'm going upstairs. I'll be right back, okay?" I called out on my way up.

I saw her nod. I could hear her pressing numbers into the phone as I took the steps two by two, up to the bedroom area.

First, I ran into Mom's room and took the dirty box with

the black gun out of her bedside drawer. I knelt down and slid it as far under the bed as I could. At least if my mother had to take a little extra time to look for it then she might not use it, and because it was still in her room she might not be too mad that I had moved it. Then I knocked on Annie's door.

"Can I come in?"

Annie looked calm, almost pleasant, like she had been having a delicious afternoon alone until now. I felt horrible telling her what had occurred on the street.

"Shit. Wow. Holy crap," Annie managed to be clear and serious through her Sudafed haze. I remember her saying, "I'm so sorry you had to see that, Kate," and she hugged me for a long time.

The sound of Mom's voice came from downstairs. "Girls, come down and talk to your mother." She sounded calm, but we knew better. "Come down, I need to talk to you."

Annie held my hand tightly as we walked down the stairs, only letting go when we got into Mom's view.

"I am going to the police station to turn myself in. I am not sure how long I will be there. Will you guys be okay if you have to spend the night alone?"

We nodded vigorously but said nothing. Annie was fifteen. I was twelve. She could play babysitter for the night.

"Good. If you need something, go to the family next door. I need you to be okay, all right?" She had become quite pale, as if the blood had been drained out of her and not the other woman.

We knew no matter what act of passion her madness induced her to perform that day, in some deep and clear part of her, she loved us.

"Listen, girls, I want you to learn something from me, okay? Don't ever expect a man to take care of you. After you are forty, there will be nothing out there for you. No man will want you. No man will take care of you, and you will have wasted your life taking care of him, only to be thrown out with the trash. Don't let what happened to me happen to you."

We both nodded. The thought that no man would take care of us, EVER, was a lot of information for a couple of emotionally weary adolescents, but we knew better than to argue anymore.

Thank God my mother did not have to spend the night in jail. I don't know why, but she was only asked to sit in a cell for a few hours to contemplate her actions while things got "worked out." Either the Newport Beach Police Department appreciated the fact she had turned herself in, or for some reason I still don't know, my father and his girlfriend didn't press charges.

The beating was to be the last of the violence for a while. At the end of that summer, Annie and I waited in the hallway of the Costa Mesa courthouse for our parents' divorce to be finalized. Mom dressed us like we were going to Christmas Mass. My black patent leather shoes felt tight on my feet. I was told I might be called as a witness against Dad for the Sunday afternoon "nap." Mom saw this event as "the big gun" that was going to get her everything she wanted, or at the very least, the Mercedes. I didn't want to testify against my dad, no matter what he did. I loved him.

The settlement was over in a few hours. Our father did not say hello to us inside the courthouse, but walked out another door, far from where we sat in our shiny shoes and pretty dresses. His shame was tangible, at least. Jacqueline Dana, no longer McClain, walked out of the courtroom door and straight to us, full of files.

"It's over. Let's go."

"Am I going to have to talk?" I asked softly.

"No."

"What happened?"

"Nothing. Let's go."

She never went into detail about what happened inside the courtroom. All we knew was she had been given full custody of us.

Dad stopped by the Condo to say goodbye. I didn't understand what was happening. Why was he saying goodbye? Were we not going to see him anymore? He looked pained and thin. We were formally asked if we wanted to spend any time with him. It wasn't a difficult answer after everything that had happened. I loved him, but it wasn't he that fed me or took me to school or shopping for clothes. It wasn't he who helped me with my homework or drove me to auditions—not once. He didn't even pay the rent most of the time. I had to be practical. Did I want to spend time with Dad the cheater, the absent, the one who spent all the money on himself and his girlfriends—the man who had provoked such extremes in our mother that she beat up his girlfriend, chopped up his gifts, and contemplated suicide? The man who made my mother so angry she drank and cried all day? The father who could not, would not, speak? I longed for him to be someone else, anybody else. I longed for him to talk—to tell me how sorry he was that he had left us, that he was going to make it all better and be there for us and help us grow up. But he didn't. He just stood there like a child himself, waiting for us to beg him to stay. I looked at my mother and Annie. Their spirits had been ravaged by his selfishness.

"I'm angry at you," I finally said, breaking the stalemate. "You hurt Mom."

He said nothing.

"I don't want to live with you and your girlfriend. I want to stay with Mom."

I watched him withdraw even further into himself. He was still wearing his courtroom suit, as if he was going to go to work that day, which seemed unlikely. He shook his head and dropped it a little, defeated and shamed, finally. I loved him so much. It killed me to tell him that he could go to hell, but I felt I had no choice. If it was him or Mom, it had to be Mom. She may have been crazy but at least she had never abandoned us.

After an awkward hug where we barely touched, he walked out the door, stuffing five hundred dollars in cash under the front door mat.

Immediately, things started looking bleak financially. I knew I had twenty thousand dollars saved from the commercials I had made. It was a tiny amount compared to the hundreds of thousands I had pulled in, but at least it was something. Somehow our mother had managed to put this money away in a private account while they sorted out the divorce. Now we needed it.

"I'm sorry, Kate. We're broke, and your asshole father gives us nothing."

I said, "fine," of course. What else could I say?

"This won't go on forever," she promised. As we walked out of the bank, she put her sunglasses on as if everyone could tell she was taking money from her child.

"It's okay, Mom, I can always make more, right? I'll make more, 'cause I'm young, right?" She stared hard at me.

"I'll pay you back. I'll talk to my father." She stopped for a second, contemplating that thought, then returned to her quick stride toward the car. "I'll figure something out."

I wanted her to be happy and was pissed at my mom's reaction. I thought, "I have rescued us! I am the hero! I should be applauded!" But Mom wasn't applauding. She just seemed serious and quiet.

"She's probably jealous because Dad liked me better," I reasoned sulkily, "but she isn't the only one who has to survive being left."

A Small Break

"Well, girls, it's time to grow up and decide what you want to do for a living," Mom announced the morning after the divorce. "I'm too old to keep doing this mothering nonsense. We are all going to have to pull our weight around here now that your dad is gone, okay? So. Whatcha' wanna do? Think about it and get back to me." With her announcement delivered, she walked out of the room.

My sister and I looked at each other.

"Jesus Christ," Annie murmured under her breath.

"What is she talking about, Anns?"

I was confused. I had done a fair amount of work already in TV, but it never felt like more than an after-school project that brought in money to help with the bills. I was used to being a bit of a circus freak at school but I hadn't considered it would become my life's work.

"She's nuts. Just ignore her," Annie whispered. "Don't tell her I said that. Wanna split my Diet Coke with me?"

"Sure. Are there any chips left?" I queried.

We rummaged in the cabinets. Dad had managed to eat

every chip in the house the last time he was around, and Mom hadn't replaced them.

Annie was pissed. "No chips! Asshole!"

"Crap," I agreed. "What else is there?"

Opening the fridge, we discovered a giant fruit salad was waiting. It would do. We hauled the huge plastic Tupperware bowl into the TV room and put it on the floor. I took my spoon and sorted through the fruit on the hunt for grapes, my favorite. They were always at the bottom.

As we munched on our snack, I flipped through the channels using my toes to turn the knob on the TV. I wondered if Mom was right—if it was time to get serious about choosing a vocation. I was about to enter eighth grade after all, almost ready for high school.

I threw out an idea. "Hey Anns...you know, if I was a Roman in the 2nd century AD, I would be married by now, maybe even having a baby!" We had recently been watching *I, Claudius*, a TV series about the fall of the Roman Empire.

"Kate, please shut up. Just keep doing what you are doing. It will all work out fine." Annie was tensing up and starting to get that look on her face that meant, "Conversation Over."

We quietly took turns fishing for grapes.

"Hey, you wanna play a game?" I asked. I thought any distraction would have been a good one. Watching my sister get mad was painful. It meant she was going to go to her room soon, shutting the door against the world, which unfortunately included me. Instead, she softened for a moment.

"No, let's go to the pool."

It was just a community pool, nothing special, but it was clean and wide and not filled with screaming kids that day. We swam next to each other doing a sideways stroke we had learned by watching old Esther Williams' movies on TV. I didn't hang onto Annie like I usually did or ask her to play "Let's Pretend We're Mermaids" at the bottom of the pool—we just swam laps back and forth. After awhile we got out, wrapping ourselves in big beach towels. We lay in the sun on the loungers until the wind picked up and it got too cold to be outside. It was a rare moment, only to be interrupted by our growing fear of Mom's rage.

Our mother had become uncomfortable with my sister and me spending time alone to do as we pleased. She said she was afraid our father might kidnap us, but I think it had more to do with her fear we would mutiny. Lest we go wandering off to the pool again, she signed us up for all kinds of "after-school activities," some of which included sewing and cake decorating classes.

Sewing was full of rules that could not be broken and measurements that had to be precise. I wanted to impale myself on the cutting scissors (something I mimed often in class when the teacher's back was turned.) The only good part was picking out our own fabric. I chose dark blue cotton with a pattern of little sheep grazing in a green field on it. Annie chose a cotton fabric of a color that could be described as "desert beige." After weeks of wrestling with the cutting board and sewing machine, we showed off our stiff looking "wrap-around" skirts to Mom.

She was so proud she toasted us with her Vodka tonic and

said, "Girls, if I've taught you anything, I have taught you this: if you can't be decorative, be useful."

The cake decorating classes she insisted on were much more fun. We pretended the chocolate icing in the bag was poop and went crazy "pooping" all over the little cake that was supposed to look like a tree log covered in plastic animals. In order to crack my sister up, I would put the icing bag up to my mouth and "eat" the "poop." Sometimes we laughed so hard we had to put our heads down on the table so the other cake decorators would stop turning around to glare at us. We made cakes that looked like giant hamburgers, cakes that looked like planets, cakes that looked like balloons...we baked and decorated those damn cakes until the thought of one more made us want to puke. It was a good thing those skirts were adjustable. We each put on about ten pounds.

Unfortunately, Mom decided to take an early holiday photo of my sister and me for a Christmas card. She insisted we come out onto the grassy hill by the community pathway and pose in Christmas sweaters with the giant teddy bear I had bought as a reward for my career efforts. It seemed like some kind of cruel joke—cake decorating all summer and now this? Pouring ourselves into red and green wool sweaters too hot for the weather and jeans too snug to close, we felt stupid and hideous. But Mom was determined. She hauled the giant stuffed bear out onto the neighborhood lawn, and putting a big Christmas ribbon around its neck, called for us to come outside and get our photo taken. Albeit silent, we went under protest.

"Stand on either side of the bear, girls. Good! Now don't look at me; look at the camera. Good! Smile! Annie! Jesus, c'mon! You look constipated!" Annie wasn't pleased with this display of her new weight. "Smile, goddamn it! It's a Christmas photo! What's wrong with you?"

I thought of the gun upstairs and froze up inside my body, smiling like a crazed psychiatric patient, my shoulders around my ears.

"It will go faster if you just do it," I whispered to Annie, our backs momentarily turned to so Mom couldn't see us talking. "Just pretend you're someone else."

Annie managed a smile for about five seconds, but it was enough. Mom got her shot.

I had a couple of interesting jobs that year. One was a TV movie starring Ann-Margret called *Who Will Love My Children?* It was based on the true story about an impoverished woman with cancer. On set I met some kids who played my siblings who later became big TV stars: Soleil Moon-Frye, who became the star of *Punky Brewster*, and Tracey Gold, one of the stars of the series *Growing Pains*. We spent a fair amount of time together. Tracey had a very outgoing personality, whereas Soleil was very quiet. I don't know if she was even five years old at the time, but on set she appeared to have no fear. Unlike those two brave and tenacious little girls, I felt shy in front of the camera—like I was sewing my role together with the few parts that I could spare.

The other job I booked was a recurring role on the series *St. Elsewhere.* I played the daughter of a nurse with breast cancer. In my first scene the nurse took my hand and put it on her breast to feel the lump. It was very odd to touch this total stranger's boob.

Why I was hired for these roles of children who lose their mothers, I did not know. Perhaps the casting directors could see something in me that I could not.

I think Mom recognized a growing vulnerability in me as well and decided I needed toughening up. The month before I started high school, she decided to send me away to a "Born Again Christian Cowboy Riding Camp." Maybe she knew I had seen too much in the last year, or maybe she had something she needed to do without me, but either way I was more than ready to have a break from the family drama and didn't care whether the camp was Christian, Buddhist, or Atheist. I'd be there for four weeks—they turned out to be life changing.

As we drove to the camp, the manicured world of Newport slowly crumbled away. Palm trees and wide, manicured lawns gave way to condos, then motor homes, then to a rougher landscape full dusty hills, coyotes, and untrimmed eucalyptus trees. As we made our way up deeper into the backcountry, the previously hidden desert of California revealed itself like a billowy hippie mistress—full of love and covered in dirt.

It was an interesting system they used at the ranch. After breakfast—a meal that consisted of cut up hot dogs in eggs or tiny boxes of sugary cereal in tiny cardboard boxes—we would be sent out for chores, which usually included raking up a lot of animal poop. If there was nothing else to do, we raked the dirt into patterns. We had to earn the right to care for the goats, cows, or horses.

After chores we went to classes to learn about the rules that made up the life of the ranch.

Rule Number One: Be the best you can be.

Rule Number Two: Your horse is smarter than you are. Don't fall off.

Rule Number Three: No chores = no lunch. No exceptions.

Rule Number Four: Jesus is our Lord and Savior and John Wayne is next in line.

Rule Number Five: No jokes about The Duke.

I liked structure. The clarity of what was expected of me was liberating. Within a week, I could name all the parts of a goat, a sheep, a cow, and a horse. Another week after that, I knew all the parts of a saddle, all the different types of bridles and their parts, and what bits to use on difficult horses. After I passed these tests, I was allowed to care for the animals.

My favorites were the goats. I loved how they waited for the kids like me who came in and milked them. The goats reminded me of the animal "rabble" that my sister and I had played with as little girls—"Teddy," "Big Dog," and the rabbits in hats and jackets. Like our stuffed animals, the goats even had a distinct pecking order. If they could talk, they would probably gossip outrageously, spit in the dirt, and shoot milk from their teats into the air just for fun.

By the third week, I earned a certificate to drive a horse and buggy down Main Street. By the fourth (and last) week, I was a good enough rider to be allowed to take a stallion and gallop all by myself to pick up the mail a half mile down the dirt path to the public road. I felt strong, accomplished, and free. The ranch people didn't talk much, but I didn't mind. I didn't want to talk. There was too much to do.

Annie and Mom came for Visitors' Day toward the end of my stay. They watched me do simple gymnastic tricks on a horse loping around in a wide circle and gallop a huge cranky brown mare through a barrel race, where I planted flags in barrels filled with dirt without losing my cowboy hat. After that, I introduced them to the goats and showed them my bunk. I hoped Mom would say I could stay there. The ranch did take in some kids as full timers.

"Well, you've certainly made yourself at home," she said, looking wildly out of place in her khakis and pearls, her light blue cotton sweater thrown over her shoulder. "I could leave you here and you'd be fine! Maybe I should!" She laughed but looked nervous.

"How's it going?" I asked Annie, already forgetting we weren't supposed to talk in front of Mom.

Annie had been forced to play "Mom's Best Friend" all summer long. I realized perhaps I should have kept my mouth shut.

"Well, Mom and I have been shopping for a new place to live. She was going to tell you later, but you might as well know now. We moved."

It would take a few more years until this sort of thing didn't shock me.

"Moved? Where?" No one had mentioned anything in their letters from home. No one even asked me how I might feel about moving. My sense of safety had just started to attach itself to the camp. I didn't want to leave, but if I had to, at least I knew I was going back to something I knew, or so I thought.

Instead of reacting, I acted. I said as nicely as I could, "Oh! Really? Where's the new house?" as if it were the most normal question in the world.

Mom piped up, seemingly happy there was to be no debate. "It's a town called Irvine—about a half-hour east from Newport. It's just the same as Newport. Well, not really. It's cheaper. Anyway, you can keep going to the same school if you want, it will just be a longer drive." I noticed she was fiddling with the toggles on her purse. "Don't worry, it's not that bad."

"Not that bad" sounded not that good.

I found out later the bank had foreclosed on the condo. My twenty thousand dollars had gone right down the toilet.

I went to bed that night and tried to burn the sounds of the country into my memory as I fell into a deep sleep.

In my dreams I was riding a big black horse, like the stallion I had ridden to the mailbox. It galloped hard through deep woods, moving quickly. I knew that the horse was taking me someplace dangerous, someplace where I knew I would gain knowledge whether I wanted it or not. Then we stopped in front of a cave. I got off the horse and went inside.

Once past the entrance I saw a long hallway. On the right were two doors. As I walked past them, I could see inside. A different kind of adventure was offered within each. In the first, I could ride in a hot air balloon up into the sky. In the second, I could go skiing down a steep hill. Men who were already on these adventures called to me, "C'mon! C'mon in!" but I didn't. They looked out of control and frightened me.

To the left there was only one door. I saw a long assembly line with a motorized rubber counter that moved in a u-shape from worker to worker. All the workers had slicked back black hair pulled tightly into a bun and wore white nurse uniforms. They looked very stern. I decided to go in.

Suddenly, I found myself on the motorized line, my body on all fours, moving from woman to woman. My pants had been pulled down around my ankles. Each woman gave me a hard, painful slap on the ass near my vagina and stimulated a place between my legs. Then the machine moved me to the next woman, where I would get another slap. It felt like a rhythm was being beaten out on me.

When I got off the assembly line, I felt much more taken apart then put together. I found myself back in the hallway. I still didn't want to go into the doors on the right, so I walked down to the very end of the hall.

There I found an old wooden door. I knew I didn't need the key. I just pushed the door open. Inside was a large room with a metal tabletop that was set on an angle. There was a very large, tall man inside. He was dressed all in black and had a mask covering his face and head. I could only see his eyes. He had a metal glove on one hand that was made of tiny chains, like some type of medieval armor.

"Lay down," he said, and I did. I spread my naked legs wide (my pants still off from the machine line beating) and tucked my feet into straps. He pulled his hand way back and slapped me between my legs. It thrilled and terrified me. The cold, hard slapping of metal against my soft, light pink skin was intensely stimulating. I could feel my vagina get wet and my nipples harden.

"But I'm a child," I said to no one. "I'm a child."

This dream recurred for years.

Escape

When I woke up, it was as if I were in a room I had never seen before. It had all my belongings in it, but they looked different, as if they had been fundamentally changed in a way I couldn't figured out.

The room felt cold but was almost blinding from the sun. "Air conditioning," I thought. I noticed there were no curtains or shades on the windows. Closing my eyes, I realized I could hear traffic from a highway nearby.

I got up and walked into the hallway. I saw three doors and stairs that led down to a level below. I knocked on what I thought might be my sister's door because it was closed.

"Annie, you in there?"

"I'M WORKING. GO AWAY." There it was—the familiar voice from behind a thousand words, a thousand facts, inside a thousand books. I must be home. But what home was this?

"Sorry, Annie."

I looked at the door and wondered if she, too, had been transferred without her willingness and was just trying to hold on by enforcing her habit of study with military discipline.

I realized then I was in the new condo. I had fallen asleep during the dark ride home from the ranch and awoke in my new room. As I walked around, I discovered the place was nothing short of horrifying. The front yard was full of old plants covered with a grimy film of traffic exhaust. The living room was musty with low ceilings and no windows, and the backyard was almost non-existent. Worst of all were the hordes of cockroaches in the kitchen that seemed to come out en-mass at night. I didn't dare go downstairs without turning on the light. They had crawled all over every bit of floor and countertop.

It wasn't as if Mom wasn't bringing in any money at all; it just wasn't enough. Back in Newport, she'd taken a job as a stockroom assistant and then quit in an outrage over "poor management." Even though she had her law degree, she didn't want to go to work as a legal secretary. She told me she was meant to be an artist and damn it if it wasn't her turn. She would start her new career by painting whimsical plaster figurines, selling them in craft shops while teaching housewives how to paint them once a week. As a result of her new vocation, dozens of tiny plaster figurines and pots of acrylic paint completely covered the kitchen counters.

My boom in income during my early years of show biz had given her and Dad the illusion that the "money train" would never stop coming in. Now that I wasn't booking as many commercials, we couldn't afford to live as we once had. We had no child support or alimony coming in from Dad. In fact, he had disappeared without a trace.

My job was to go on auditions and get work. In the meantime, I could have given a shit about anything else. I wanted to get a good tan and listen to the radio. It was high time, I decided, to make some attempts at being a normal teenager.

As we survived our first year in the Cockroach Condo, things seemed to offer the hope that normalcy might be within reach. Distracted by her projects, Mom allowed me to go to a friend's house in Newport after school until she was done with her class. Mandy's house was the best. Her parents were still married and her sisters were always asking about fun stuff—boys, bands, movies, and clothes. I have to admit, sometimes it was hard to stand in my friend's room and see all the "appropriate" accoutrements belonging to a newly teenaged girl: the lacy pillows and filmy curtains whispering of romance, slow crushes, and makeout sessions to come. Her stuffed animals were carelessly flung around, and new makeup was left open on a mirrored dresser. My room was spotless, almost stark in comparison. Annie and I had to keep our beds made and rooms clean or Mom might lose her shit and pull all our clothes out of the closet like when we were little kids.

"At least our mom is never dull," I remember thinking ruefully.

During a sleepover, we snuck out and met up with some boys on the beach. It was fun, at first. We found an empty fire pit with a few logs left in it, and someone managed to get a fire going. We sat around the warm flames in a circle and sipped big Australian beers that one of the boys had snuck out of his parents' fridge. There wasn't much conversation; we mostly watched the fire burn down and listened to the ocean roar. It was "all cool" until the one African-American boy in the whole school put his arm around me.

It seemed like a pushy move because I didn't really know him, but I liked that he liked me. He was cute and at least he wasn't a director or one of those weird producers who always seemed to get too close. As I considered whether this was cool with me or not, I felt a strange ripple go through the group. One of the other boys, a junior, made a sudden show of being interested in me. He picked me up and started to carry me off like we were going to go make out somewhere. I remember screaming and laughing. I felt beautiful because it seemed the boys were fighting over me. But they weren't. I looked back over the shoulder of the boy who was carrying me away and saw the caramel colored boy had been left sitting by the fire. Only then did I realize what had really happened. I had been removed from his grasp.

I knew in that moment it was something about the color of his skin that made the other boy pull me away from him. There was nothing wrong with him—he wasn't weird, or rude, or funny looking—he just had brown skin. I wished so much that I had said something in the moment, but my own feelings of insecurity and desperate desire to belong overrode my courage. I wasn't alone. Everyone pretended that what had happened actually hadn't.

The next day at school, instead of doing nothing, I decided to hate the other boys, hate them and ignore them at school, to show them that I "got what they did," and didn't like it. It didn't make any difference. They didn't care about me, really. I could choose my side, but it would be a side of one. As it turned out, the African-American boy didn't care what I thought, either. When I said "hi" to him in the hall that day, he put his head down and looked the other way, as if I didn't exist.

After that experience, I began to hate the whole school and all the preppy, privileged kids in it. "They are so sheltered," I thought. "They have no idea what it's like to be afraid to go home." I wondered how Annie had made it through four years at that high school and then I remembered the books. Annie was there but not there. That's how she survived the divorce, moving, teenage pressures, the insanity of our parents, and the privileged white world we were privy to but not a part of—there but not there.

When it finally dawned on me how my sister had survived, I began to think about how I might escape, too. I wasn't able to focus the way Annie could and just read all day, but I had show business. I didn't really know what acting was, but I knew I could acclimate to anything. Auditioning didn't teach me how to act; it taught me how to survive an awkward situation. I needed something where I could act all the time—some place that wasn't my school. One day, while looking in the local paper, I saw an advertisement for a theatrical production at the local community theater that was starting up in the summer. It looked like a good place to start my journey OUT.

I snuck up on my mom when she was painting in the kitchen and laid out my plan.

"So...Mom...there's this play I saw an ad for...um...I think I need to do, you know, like, some more acting work so I can get better at it so I can make more money, you know? I was thinking, maybe I can audition for this play? It's a musical. I think I could get it since I tap dance. Do you think that would be okay?" Mom looked at me like I had two heads.

"A play? Does it pay anything?"

I looked down at the paper. "Yeah, it does." I thought quickly. "The shows are on the weekends so I could still audition. The whole commitment is, like, three weeks, I think."

The income from my work was essential to our well-being. I knew this but forced myself to believe instead that this was all momentary—that there was a secret fund somewhere where money had been put aside for my college education. I couldn't linger on the idea that there might not be anything left after the hundreds of the rides up and back to Los Angeles wedged in between my parents' madness and whatever school I could cram into my head. It was too awful to contemplate. I couldn't ask Mom for the truth unless I wanted to hear a guilt-laden tirade, so I pushed it aside and focused on the long game of getting work.

Mom took a big sigh. "Okay, Kate. Do it if you want. Annie's gotta tour some colleges this summer, so at least a play would keep you busy." I watched her chew on her paintbrush for a moment. Then she dipped the tip of the brush into a pot of red acrylic paint and began to contemplate the Christmas hat of a small ceramic squirrel.

The only word I heard was "college."

I hadn't thought of Annie actually leaving. If she had to travel to tour a college, then that meant she was thinking of going to college somewhere other than nearby. All of a sudden, it hit me. I realized Annie's studying had really been for physical escape, not just mental survival. All those years she had been planning to leave and get away—leaving me all alone with Mom.

"ANNIE!" I screamed up the stairs toward her room. "AN-NIE! WHERE ARE YOU?" I could hear the shower running and barged in. "ANNIE!"

"What the hell, privacy please!" She turned off the water and grabbed a towel.

I didn't care about her dignity. "Are you leaving? Mom said you're leaving. Are you leaving for school?"

"What do you think, dummy?" She wasn't going to sugarcoat it for me. I had been in the movies and received lots of positive attention as "the talented one" while she had to suck it up as "the smart one." It hadn't been fun for her, but at the moment I couldn't think about that.

"Where are you going?"

"Look. I got into three schools. I have to choose the right one or I won't get into a good Master's program." There had been conversations going on that I clearly had not been privy to. My head was spinning. Three schools? Master's program? What the hell?

"I'm going away, Kate. I have to get out of here. And don't tell Mom I said that." She pulled on her robe over her towel, wrapped a second one around her hair, and left the bathroom in a huff.

I followed her like a puppy into the tiny room that had become her inner sanctum. It was the size and width of a prison cell and covered with books. I had never seen this side of my sister before. Who was this person?

"When will you leave? Will you come home?" I was starting to use the "high voice" I slipped into when I got scared. "Are you coming back?"

Once she got her slippers on, she softened, but only slightly. She couldn't take on my panic. The pressure to succeed and be our mother's friend in all things had whipsawed her between her own need for our mother's warmth and her need to protect herself from Mom's cruelty and foolishness.

She sat me down on her bed and hugged me. "Don't worry, little mouse. I'll be home for the holidays, you'll see."

As my tears fell down my sister's robe, I knew she was lying. Annie would get as far away as she could and come home as little as possible. If she could fly to the moon, build a fort, and live there reading books forever, she would have. I couldn't blame her. I couldn't blame her at all.

That year as I tap-danced and sang my way through a month of summer, my sister disappeared into the ether. Just like that. Books, clothes, shoes—everything but her desk and her twin bed were gone. Without her there, I tried hard to disappear into the world of the play. It wasn't too difficult when I was on stage. There were too many costume changes to think about what was going to happen next. There was only the next line, next step, or the next song. When it was over, I had a glimmer of hope that I had indeed found the place I could find relief. As long as I had acting, I had escape. That summer it was the part of "Ruby" in the 1940's musical *Dames at Sea*.

After Mom returned from settling my sister into a respected university halfway across the country, she made an announcement.

"Looks like it's just you and me, kid! Time to downsize!"

I sure as hell didn't mind saying goodbye to the musty Cockroach Condo we were barely managing to pay for, but when she showed me where we would be moving to I began to think that perhaps I was being punished for something. This condo was located in what was clearly one of the more dilapidated developments in Irvine. It had a backyard that smelled like Yak ass due to some kind of tree that dropped its pebbly fruit all over the eight-by-five foot cement space laughingly referred to as a "backyard." I dubbed it "The Shit Tree." The front yard didn't stink, but it had no plants. On either side of the walkway the dirt was littered with cigarette butts.

The kitchen had greasy orange appliances we had to wash down with ammonia and hot water. Since it had only two bedrooms, I would have to share a room with Annie when she came home for the summer (assuming she would come home.) I pursed my lips like my sister used to and shook my head. I couldn't imagine the sparkling girls from Newport visiting this place. If the last condo was iffy, this one was off limits. I wouldn't be able to take the pity. Three words rolled over and over in my head as I stared at the living room floor.

GOLD. SHAG. CARPETING.

Dark brown and golden fibers mixed together to look more or less like baby shit mixed with diarrhea.

Mom had meanwhile moved on from petite ceramics to larger decorative wooden shapes. "Rabbit in Clover" and "Lounging Kitty" plaques began to stack up in the kitchen. A giant rack of acrylic paint sat on the counter and coffee cups overflowed with paintbrushes. She would sit there for hours lovingly painting flowers and fat cherubs around the smiling faces of animals. Once a little puppy dog with ribbons around its ears appeared with my name on it in my bedroom. A gift. I sat and stared at it, wondering if I was going to have to haul this piece of crap around with me for the rest of my life in order not to hurt my mother's feelings.

"Thanks so much, Mom. I love it." I lied, giving her a big hug. It was a good opening to hit her up with a new idea I had. "So hey…um… I think I want to change schools." It was only two weeks before the fall semester started, but things had declined too far in our world. The Newport girls could not see Mister Puppy and the gold shag carpet. That just wasn't gonna happen.

"Huh? How's that?" She was surprised. "Now?"

"Yeah. The high school in Irvine has a good theater program. Maybe it will help me get more work." I had learned the keyword to getting what I wanted. Work.

"Oh, God. Yeah. Okay, good thought. Um, I'll call someone; just give me a second. I want to finish this flower. Paint is wet. Wet paint." After Miss Kitty got her roses, I changed schools.

We might have been cutting costs and coupons, but at least we still had the car. It was our last status symbol, and we clung to it like a life raft. I was grateful that she could drop me off and pick me up from school in that car. Carefully cradling her day-long coffee cup between her knees, Mom could shift her beloved tan Mercedes through its truck-like gears without spilling a drop. After a full day with strangers, she had become like a war buddy—we had seen some days others could only imagine.

"Didn't we used to have a dog, Mom?" I asked her one time on the drive home. "What happened to Dinah?"

"Oh, you know. Your father." Whatever that meant.

I looked out the window. "Why doesn't he call? Doesn't he want to see me?" My eyes darted along the sidewalk filled with mica that led to my school. It sparkled, reminding me of the sidewalk in Newport the day Mom had beat up his girlfriend. I thought about Dad's shoes, similarly glinting in the sun as he walked away. "Do you think he'll ever show up again?"

Mom pulled her cup from between her knees and took a slurp. "Things are better this way."

I took a long look at my mother. I noticed red dots starting to form around her nose.

"Can we get a cat?" No, Dad, so maybe a cat would be okay.

"Let's wait on that."

No cat. No sister. No dog. No Dad. Just Mom.

Shit.

"When's Annie coming home?" I began to eye my mother's red nose with suspicion. I wondered if she was keeping our family hidden away somewhere so she could have their full attention all to herself. It didn't occur to me her drinking and crying might have been wearing on her.

"Soon. Christmas."

She pulled around the corner to our section of identical shitty condos. Ours was the third white one with the brown garage on the left. I could only tell it was ours by the number "3" nailed into the wall. Maybe our neighbors' shit tree was different, but I doubted it. The whole neighborhood stank.

"Hey, what happened to our Barbies?"

"Garage sale."

"Board games?"

"Same. I asked you and you said you didn't want them, remember?"

I didn't. My mind wandered back to my father. If she could have sold him at a garage sale, I bet she would have.

"Do you think Dad will ever come back?"

She sighed one of her deep irritated sighs. "Kate. He wasn't a good father. He wasn't a good man. You are better off without him in your life."

"Doesn't he love me anymore?"

"I don't know, honey. I think your dad only loves himself."

No matter what had happened or what she said, no matter what kind of a cowardly douche bag he might have actually been, I simply couldn't grasp the idea that my dad might not love me. I began to believe that all this moving might be my mom running from him. It had been almost three years since I had seen him with no letter or call—at least not that I knew about.

"Did he ever send a letter?" I had to find out if she was hiding something.

"No letters." She stopped the car in the driveway. "Now look, kid. We are better off now, no matter what. He was a shit and now he's gone. I'm sorry it sucks." Then she looked hard at her aching adolescent child and saw something she had to fix. "Let's go inside and talk."

After that, every day when I got home from school, I sat down with Mom and "talked." It wasn't happy chit-chat about boys or homework. It was serious and it was about Dad. Bad Dad. I cried sometimes, but most of the time I felt scared to say what I really felt. After a month of this, I just wanted to go back to my room, but her feeling was "you started it" and we were going to finish, or else.

"If you don't want to talk, we will sit here and look at each other until this father shit is over, and that is all there is to it." Mom was nothing if not resolute.

I tried to apply myself to my homework, but I couldn't focus. I knew I had to keep my grades up high enough to maintain my entertainment industry work permit, required by the state of California for child actors. However, that year my grades danced around the alphabet. I just couldn't get myself to care about anything.

At Christmas, Annie came home pissed off and tired from the stress of college. She didn't want to do anything but lie in the sun and watch TV. I had never heard her so opinionated about everything. Once she was free from our mother, a whole submerged personality began to reveal itself. I suggested we do something we both liked, swimming, so I could get to know her again. She agreed. While we waited for Mom to leave to teach her class (so she wouldn't see us in our bathing suits and make bitchy comments about our bodies or ganging up on her), we made instant iced tea in plastic glasses. Even though the granules of the tea stuck to my ice cubes, I liked that Annie and I had a mutual task.

Apparently, almost every condo development in southern California has a community pool. Ours was no different, but this one was filled with what I lovingly dubbed "The Lizard People." These were elderly people who did nothing but lie in the sun and rub themselves with oil until they were a dark brown, much browner than the Mexicans. Why all white people wanted to be tan but not Mexican or African-American made not a bit of sense to me. As we lay down on our towels, I noticed my sister looking cross and irritated in her fraying black swimsuit.

"How was college?" I asked, genuinely curious.

Annie gave a deep sigh and looked at me like I was an idiot. She spoke slowly. "Very competitive. You have to speak up or they will shoot you down, you understand?"

I shook my head.

"No." I was not going to give in to the idea that adult life outside of my mother's control was harder than life in it. "Isn't everybody nicer?"

She picked up her tea and slurped, "You don't understand. It's not about being nice. School is a competition, and if you don't win, you lose. If you lose, you are a loser, stuck here in the shit part of Irvine, get it?" She lay back on her towel, exhausted. "Don't pressure me, Kate. I'm tired."

I was stunned into silence. "At least you aren't living full-time in the shag-carpeted shithole like I am," I thought. "At least you got out. At least you have a chance." I didn't think, "You earned it." We never celebrated any of our accomplishments, other than me making money. Even then, it was a minor affair—a box of donuts or takeout. It didn't occur to me there was anything wrong with this. It was just the way our family operated.

We lay there for a half-hour, enjoying our moment of independence. As I lay there, I tried to imagine what it would be like if I had the little yellow sports car that our neighbor across the street drove. I imagined myself driving over the hills of Irvine and back to Laguna Beach, where some of my childhood friends were now getting their first cars. I had asked my mom if we could buy a car like our neighbor's so I could drive, but she said we couldn't afford the insurance.

I looked over at Annie and wondered if she had ever thought about driving. She was eighteen and there had been no discussion of such a thing. I don't even remember her sixteenth birthday—if we had a party or what—and there was never any discussion of cars. She must have wanted one, but I don't remember it ever coming up.

I looked over at her. She was getting burned.

"You wanna go in?"

There wasn't going to be any more relevant conversation today, not without getting her pissed off. She went back to school after a week in order to get a jump on classes, or so she said. I didn't want her to go, but it was up to me to figure out how to make the jump to independence, as she had accomplished.

Iris Burton called not too long after that. She had decided there was a problem with my name.

Her years of smoking gave her voice a croak like a toad with a cold, "Look. Honey. I have this girl, Katie McSwain. She's getting a lot of work, honey, and you guys are getting confused. So can you change your name, darling? Can you do that? Let me know." *Click.* She hadn't waited for a response.

I wondered why Katie McSwain (or whomever she was) wasn't asked to change her name, but guessed it had something to do with the fact I wasn't booking as much work as I used to.

I couldn't leave Iris, not yet, as she was still my key to escape. So my mom and I sat down at the local Bob's Big Boy Diner, where I doodled some names on a napkin.

"Did she say I had to change my whole name, or just part of my name?"

Mom shrugged. I could tell she felt a little bit bad for me.

"You don't have to do it, you know. We can try to find you another agent."

I kept doodling.

"How about I just change the spelling of my name? Maybe just my first name?"

My mom look worried but nodded. "Sounds reasonable."

I tried "K-a-t-y," but it was too close to "K-a-t-i-e," and I wasn't quite ready for strangers to call me "Kate." It was too personal.

"How about a 'C'?" "C-a-t-y? No, that looks weird. How about C-a-d-y? Is that an actual name? Wasn't there a writer named Cady?" My napkin was filling up with little "c's" and "k's" and "t's" and "d's." I looked questioningly at my mom who, because she had gone to college, had to know things I did not know—like the names of famous writers.

"I think so. Yes, I think there was a very famous Cady. Uh, Elizabeth Cady something. She fought for women, I think." I wished she talked more about this type of thing.

"Okay. Well, that's it then. C-a-d-y. But I'm keeping my last name, okay?"

It was funny she let me keep that little reminder of my dad. I wondered if it had something to do with my sister and I needing to stay related somehow, or some legal reason, or if it was more because if I changed my last name, a residual check might not be able to find me.

My work had the unfortunate effect of keeping me completely ostracized at school. No one my age in Newport or Irvine was "on TV" or "in the magazines," except for Robert MacNaughton, who was three years older than me and famous for having played one of the kids in Steven Spielburg's *E.T.* He had a younger sister close to my age, but we did not hang out with his family.

I realize now the reason my mom probably kept away from other professional moms with actor kids was to hide the issue with my money. If anyone turned her in to the unions, she could've gone to jail, and I think she knew it.

Halfway into sophomore year at my new high school, University High, I booked one big, well-paying commercial—a Maybelline ad—after which the company decided to also do a magazine shoot. In addition, they would use my photo for all the billboards and placards that were put up in drugstores across the country. It meant big money.

At the time of the commercial shoot, I had bleached blonde hair that was naturally wavy, like a perfect little Maybelline girl. There was nothing I had to do but stay exactly the same and show up when it was time to take the picture. However, a week before the shoot, Mom took me to the hairdresser to have my hair permed. My hair wasn't as wavy as it used to be, and she thought it needed some "oomph." The beautician at the cheap salon we went to left the solution in too long, and the curls came out way, way too tight. I looked like a sheep.

"Oh," my mother said.

"It was an accident!" the hairdresser who screwed up said. "We thought you wanted it that way!"

I looked at them like they were nuts. They had clearly forgotten I was at the sink.

"You look like you have an Afro," my friends said later at school.

"Who did that to you?" Annie asked me at home.

"I look like Christopher Atkins in the movie *The Blue Lagoon*," I said to the mirror alone in the bathroom. "With tits."

I tried to brush it out and make myself look normal, but it just made it worse. I ended up looking like the bride of Frankenstein. It was too short to cut any further. The only recourse was to shave my head. I avoided looking in the mirror. Instead I looked at my mom. It was her idea for me to get a perm. She knew that if Iris Burton found out, she would scream at us both in her "New York Way" and probably fire me. So we decided not to tell her.

The photo shoot for the Maybelline ad was in Dallas, Texas. When I walked onto the set, the hairdresser gasped.

"Wha-at ha-appened to-o you-u, honey? What ha-appened to-o your ha-a-ir?" She was a nice, young southern lady with a job to do. I didn't realize my showing up like an electrocution victim was putting her job on the line as well.

I whispered, "They screwed it up at home." I begged, "Can you help?"

God bless her, she took mercy on me. "Sit back, honey. Let's see what we can do." For one hour she massaged my head and pulled at my hair with some magic product until the curls budged a bit. She went over to the photographer and whispered in his ear and he nodded. They put me in brightly colored shirts and slapped a Walkman in my hand.

"Pretend like you hear your favorite music," they said. "Pretend you are the most gorgeous girl in school."

Damn, if I wasn't acting then. I felt so guilty for showing up and putting their whole campaign on the line. As it turned out, the hairdresser convinced the advertising people this was the hot new hair-do of the '80's, god bless her.

Looking back, it's hard to believe that campaign didn't pay enough to keep us from going underwater, but it didn't. In fact, only one year into the Gold Shag Shit Tree Condo, money was so tight my mom suggested we move to a block of tiny apartments directly across from the high school, next to the Taco Bell, which would have been one step too far toward a humiliation I couldn't handle. It made me really, really angry.

"Didn't I make a lot on that Maybelline commercial, Mom?" I asked her in the car on the way home from looking at rooms half the size as the ones we now occupied. "What happened to that?"

My mom chewed her lip and glanced down at her hands, "Well, honey, it's gone. Art doesn't pay that well, you know."

"ART? WHAT ART? WHAT FUCKING ART?" I pursed my lips tightly so I couldn't say what I was thinking.

My mother was sinking into an abyss of cookie dough and indecision. Something had to be done. I thought of the axe.

"Why don't we sell the car? Isn't it valuable or something?" I might as well have suggested she sell her body.

"Kate, this is the last goddamn thing I have from your father that is worth anything, and I will be good goddamned if I part with it, you understand? If we have nothing else, we have the car."

I wanted to say, "Oh, the car I paid for?" but blocked it from my mind before it could fester. Then I wanted to say, "Why don't you ask your family for help?" But I knew that if the car was off limits, mentioning my mother's family was like lighting a bomb, although it was clear my grandfather was helping with Annie's education. I guess that was different and fell into an acceptable category. How exactly, I wasn't sure, but it seemed since I could pay the rent, my mom didn't have to tell her father that she wasn't managing to provide for her children. This thought pushed my buttons. Suddenly, I realized I had a card I could play.

"Mom, I work my ass off. I am NOT moving into one of the apartments across from the high school. That is NOT happening." As soon as it was out of my mouth, I wished I hadn't said it. In fact, I wished I hadn't said anything. She swiftly pulled the car over, turning her attention to me, as best as her hundred-and-seventy-five pound, five-foot-two body could in the front seat of the Mercedes, to give me the full blast of her shame.

"Kate. I am sorry. I am SO GODDAMN SORRY life is not what you wanted it to be, but if you don't like it, you can goddamn well DO something about it. You're fifteen. I'm forty-five. No one is going to hire me. No one is sure as shit going to marry me. I'm old, I'm fat, and past my sell-by date."

Now the tears started. I began to dig around for an unused napkin from McDonald's stuffed into a crack in the seat.

"You wanna go home and live with my FATHER? We

could do that you know—go live in Butt Fuck, Illinois. But you won't have show business. You'll get stuck there, trust me. Stuck in the middle of nowhere—pregnant and fat and stupid. Is that what you want? Pregnant, fat, and stupid? 'Cause we can do that."

For some reason, the way my mother put it, Illinois was the worst hell imaginable, but she was two seconds from packing up the entire house and calling it quits.

"It's okay. It's OKAY, Mom. We'll figure something out. We don't have to move to Illinois. I'm sorry. I'll get a job. I'll do something."

As luck would have it, the new high school I had moved to didn't completely suck. I was invited out with a couple of nice girls to a party in one of the houses on the hill where real homes sat—houses that didn't look alike, with big trees that didn't smell like shit. I usually passed on such invites—it was better to stay safe in the condo and watch TV and not risk another embarrassing session of people asking me why I looked so bad in real life when I looked so good on TV, but all the recent fighting with my mother had been so depressing I decided I might as well go. It couldn't get any worse. Maybe a party with strangers was just the escape I needed.

The party was large, loud, and full of teenagers. Everyone seemed wildly self-conscious and horny. My new friends took me up to one of the bedrooms where other girls were gathered around a magazine. The room was dark but pretty. Lush pillows were thrown willy-nilly around the room for everyone to sit on, hug, or fart into. It was as if they couldn't care less about their parents. They wanted something else and they were looking at it. They were looking at a picture of me.

"Hey, I heard this is you. Is this you?" One of the girls asked nicely. She had a smile like a shark.

I stood there and waited for the inevitable criticism, "Why don't you look like that in real life?" followed by a huge laugh, but it didn't come.

"Hello-o? Is this picture in the magazine you?"

It was my Maybelline ad. The ad that paid so much money—money that was gone.

"Yeah," I shrugged.

I wasn't going to tell them the whole story. I was glad they weren't making fun of me, so I burped up some bullshit like, "I got a commercial and they wanted me to do the ad campaign, so, you know, I did it." I always tried to downplay my work so the inevitable jealousy that would come could be countered with some horror story from the front lines of show business. I didn't enjoy being envied.

I still don't.

The pretty girl with the white teeth looked pleased. "I think that's so cool. You look so pretty. I wish my mom would get me in a magazine. Do you think your mom would talk to my mom and tell her how to do it?"

And there it was. Now I knew why I had been invited to the party. Four teenage girls were smiling and batting their Maybelline mascara-ed, blue pencil-rimmed eyes at me, like they were already at the audition. The very thought of my mother talking to one of their mothers made me want to run out the door screaming with my hair on fire. I knew my mom could be nice at first, but she had a short shelf life as a friend.

Inevitably she'd start talking about the divorce and get emotional. After a few lunches with their moms, she would call me with some conspiracy theory as to why some mom had REALLY called her in the first place and go on about being persecuted or "purposely humiliated in her own home." It would all end with my mom screaming at some well-meaning, well-tended married woman in some public place—something I wanted to avoid like the plague.

So I lied.

"Sure. I'll ask her to call." I needed a night without drama, and if a lie bought it, then so be it. The girls screamed, giggled, and rolled around the bed.

"I'm gonna be a movie star one day, you'll see," said the pretty one, "and all the boys will wanna fuck me!" This brought on howls of wild screaming and more shrieking and giggling. I stood there bewildered.

"Fuck?" I thought, "Does somebody want to fuck me because I'm in a magazine?" I could not make the connection. All I knew was "magazine equaled money plus people acting weird around me." I knew older people, like show-biz people, wanted to fuck me, but guys my age? They always seemed scared of me. The very few at school that genuinely wanted to know me, I couldn't stand hanging around too long. I couldn't take the pity.

Finally, somebody pounded on the door—the pretty one's big brother—and shouted through the lock. "If you don't shut up, I'm gonna sick the friggin' dog on you, skank! There are seniors here, okay? Try not to be SUCH an asshole!"

He was cute and brown-eyed and could have cared less about the screaming, really. He had buddies to impress.

I opened the door and smiled. "Sorry. Got any beer?"

He did. And he had friends, too. One of them was cute and asked for my number and just like that, I had a real boyfriend—a boyfriend who lived in a condo like I did, who liked to party, make out, get a tan, and not think almost as much as I did. While with him, I found that after a couple of beers, wine coolers, or shots of somebody's dad's tequila, I could sing, scream, or be as loud as I wanted and nobody seemed to mind. Alcohol gave me the confidence to sneak into the community pool area at night with my friends to do back flips off the diving board. While drunk at the prom, I discovered the joys of shoplifting: I stole a napkin holder (for no particular reason) from the diner by sticking it under my dress and holding it between my knees as I walked out. While inebriated, I could throw myself fearlessly into life and be caught in the understanding arms of another teenager.

It lasted the summer. In the fall, when I became a junior, I dumped him and found a new boyfriend. I didn't want to fall in love and make love yet, and he did. Suddenly, boys were like beers—fun, fast, and interchangeable—and I was riding the experience like a roller coaster. I didn't care about anything anymore. I couldn't. There had been too much change, too much hurt, too much loss, too much information, too much pressure... I desperately needed an "out" and drinking became that "out." I was so drunk for the school Winter Formal dance that my new boyfriend had to carry me for the official "couples photo" we were supposed to take back to our parents to show them what good little citizens we were growing up to be. We had done shots of tequila, followed by glasses of champagne that my preppy and wild boy toy had brought, so standing up straight had become virtually impossible. I liked him a lot but felt no real joy. I wasn't even attracted to him that much, although I knew I should be. He was considered to be a real catch. My idea for our relationship was to feel as little as possible by drinking as much as possible and then try to feel something impossible by doing something incredibly outrageous I would never do otherwise. I certainly didn't feel any love and doubted if he did either. I think we were both just scratching at passion, for something to take us away from whatever was waiting at home—even if for him it was just boredom and homework. I broke up with him a week after the dance.

"Boys are just there to practice kissing anyway," I thought. "Nothing more."

There was one guy who did seem to want more. I met him at Balboa beach. Balboa in the summer was filled with college students driving their cars, riding their bikes and skateboards, and enjoying freedom from parental supervision. Kites bounced up high in the sky, and surfers flipped up and down off the waves like grasshoppers.

While visiting Balboa with a girlfriend, I saw a man and his friend barbecuing in the front yard of a house one block off the beach. It was a cute little pink summer rental with a yard in the front and a kitchen that smelled like margaritas and girls' panties. He and his friend encouraged my friend and me to come inside and talk. We all had drinks and eventually made out. My girlfriend went into the back room with the friend. I waited for a half hour, then started knocking on the bedroom door, making excuses about leaving so we could get out of there without either one getting into too much trouble.

After that experience, the man kept calling and wanting to see me. I began to wonder if he was falling in love with me. He seemed like he came from a nice family. He said he played tennis professionally and had some money and a car. I started to fantasize about how he might take care of me so I wouldn't have to live with my mom or drive to Los Angeles anymore. I kept meeting up with him at his house, kept lying down on the foldout sofa with him for heavy make-out sessions. I finally had to say, "I'm sorry. I'm fifteen and I'm a virgin. I'm not ready." I thought if he really loved me, he would wait or at least keep trying to get me to relax enough to let him in there, but instead he just stopped calling.

It was my first real heartbreak from a man other than my father. And just like with my dad, I thought if I had, he would have taken me away from my insane life with my mom.

As I think about it now, I don't think it was really "love" that broke my heart—it was a chance to get away from my mother that I missed out on because I wasn't willing to put out for it.

I remember thinking, "Clearly, freedom is more expensive than I thought," as I leaned against the wall of the condo outside my room to contemplate whether or not I had regrets. I thought about my bedroom inside and how my stuffed animals still covered my little twin bed that lined up next to my sister's. "If freedom costs me my pride, maybe pride isn't worth having. But I just can't give it away yet." I kicked the wall. "Not just yet, goddamn it."

As I contemplated my options, I began to form what

felt like a solid plan in my mind to help me get away from my mother faster. It wasn't a man I needed—it was money. I just had to make enough money. If I had enough money, then maybe I could give some to my mother—enough for her to get her own business started—and then I'd just have to have enough left to leave her and start MY life over some place else. I couldn't count on the boys to rescue me. "They just take what they want, and if they don't get it, they leave, just like Dad," I thought. "Men can't be counted on for help." Their attention always came at a cost too high to live with. I realized I'd have to do it myself.

Then I had an idea. I couldn't stay in Irvine. If I did, there was no way I was going to move forward, no way I was going to make money or get more jobs. I was going down a rabbit hole of drinking and partying, and I knew if I didn't stop, I'd be trapped by it.

The next day I sat down with my mom and tried to convince her that a move to Los Angeles could allow me to focus on show business full time, AKA, making money. I would finish my junior year at some L.A. high school and then take the GED test, allowing me to completely focus on work.

After a few moments of concern for my future and some serious consideration for the painted wooden rocking horse she was now getting ready to sell, her face went through a strange transformation. It started out heavy at first, her eyebrows scrunched and disapproving and her mouth pursed; then it somehow lightened and became wider. Her eyebrows went up and with it her whole demeanor, as if some cloud in her mind parted and a whole new world had opened up to her.

"Now, you know this is your choice to do this. I can always do something as degrading as going to work for my father," she qualified, yet again, the steamed milk from her coffee filling the room with the smell of baby. "I'll have to give up teaching art for a while. I can't commute to Orange County from Los Angeles to teach, you know. That's too far. I'll have to go back to school, learn something new. You sure you want to do this?"

I nodded. Whatever. It wasn't like she was pulling the cart for us.

"Okay, then! It will be like we are roommates! Sisters! Only I am your mother and you are the child—don't forget that. Other than that, well, fuck it, right? How old are you now? Well, you're old enough to get to work, right? That's what they did in the Depression!"

"I want to, Ma. I want do this. I need to get out of here. This place—this place isn't working, Mom. I'm drinking too much, you know that, and my grades suck." I was pretty unsure of anything but the need to change everything.

"Yeah," she nodded and pursed her lips, thinking back to when she was a sitting on a headstone smoking a cigarette— about what happened when she wasn't allowed to live as she felt she needed.

"Okay. Let's go."

Back when we were in Newport during the divorce, there had been some talk of moving to Portugal—enough talk that I began to imagine myself actually living there. It seemed like a fascinating and exciting idea. I pictured myself getting a deep tan and wearing a lot of colorful clothes, beads, and woven sandals.

"Hey, by the way…why didn't we ever move to Portugal?"
The whole possibility had put in my mind the idea that if we
moved, my whole life could change—that even who I was inside
could be different.

"Did you ask about Portugal?"

I hadn't realized I had said it aloud. I looked at my mom,
afraid for a moment.

"Um, did I?"

"Yeah. I just couldn't see myself there," she said, coffee
cup firmly in her grip as her free hand guided the paintbrush
along one last wooden board, this one of a cat sleeping in a
laundry basket. "Too risky."

"I was just thinking, maybe L.A. will be like what we
thought Portugal would be. A new start."

My mother looked at me with love. Finally, I got it. "A
new start. Yes, Kate. It will be."

The Human Life Variety Act

W̶e didn't have the money to get an apartment in Los
Angeles right away, so my mom called up a generous Christian family whom she had befriended
when we were little kids in Glendale. After one phone call, a
few of them came over to help us move our stuff into storage.
Looking like giant Norwegian Tree Huggers clad in overalls
and tie-dyed shirts, the Christian Clan of Goodness packed us
up and carried us out of the shag-shit condo in two blinks of an
owl. The next day we were unpacking our two suitcases inside
their guest room just a couple of blocks from where I was born.
It was a nice full circle. It was our second chance, our "do-over,"
starting at zero.

Despite the embarrassment of accepting help, I felt safe
there, and I hadn't felt that way in a long while. The house was
filled with family photos, televisions, and big comfy furniture.
Unlike us, they had never moved. There were knitted pothold-
ers from some grandma, early 80's posters of Michael Jackson
and Prince still hanging on the mostly grown children's bedroom walls, and even an organ for practicing music for Sunday

church. Every night they had giant dinners with the whole family (two sisters, one brother, one brother-in-law, father, mother, boyfriend, and us) hunkered around the table, praying over plates that overflowed with peas and carrots, meat, and potatoes. I looked around and tried not to attach myself to any of it: I just made a quick mental note that this was what normal looked like—something I hoped to know one day. I found myself working harder at my homework than I ever had, as if I had to create a new backup plan in case show business didn't work out after all.

My mother gave her best by spending long hours talking to Faith, the mother and head of the household, about whatever problems she seemed to be having at the time. At first it appeared like they were having the usual girl talk, but I soon became aware it was far more than that.

"It won't be long, I promise, just till the next check comes in. My father is sending us something," she lied. "I'm fucking... sorry, Faith...sorry, sorry." My mom had a problem not swearing when she was angry. "If my asshole ex-husband hadn't left us with nothing, we wouldn't be in this position."

Faith was quite possibly the most patient and charitable woman on the planet, but Mom liked to make a drama out of everything. I sometimes think she acted that way in order to make her presence more acceptable to others. As if the bigger the drama, the more people would leave her alone when it came to the little things—things that mattered far more, like how she took care of her kids. As part of her show and in deference to my mother's self-appointed position of "producer-of-all-things-that-affected-my-life," I would sometimes sing after supper. Literally.

"Look, look, look to the rainbow. Follow it over the hill and stream..."

"Isn't she talented? Isn't she lovely?"

My mother and Faith would chatter to everyone after my little show about what a star I was or was going to be, and the whole family would kindly applaud and act impressed—even if they weren't. I wondered if I made them feel bad because they weren't as comfortable as I was standing up in front of others, but I couldn't tell them I had to perform. It wasn't a choice— it's how I had been trained and what I had to give. They didn't have to sing or dance because their home was safe and their beds were guaranteed. Soon enough, whatever insecurity they might have had turned into pity for our plight, and the milk of their human kindness flowed forth once again. Somehow my mother knew exactly how this all worked and was working it just as fast and as far as she could.

Our new home was discovered about the same time as a residual check arrived in the mail. I was disappointed to leave, but it was probably for the best. My mom had pointed out just enough of Faith's husband's faults that she was making other members of the family tense. They knew their problems and didn't need a dissenter stirring the pot.

We chose an apartment on Riverside Drive, stuck between the 5 and the 134 freeways. Two small two-story buildings faced a wide center courtyard designed to reflect a somewhat romanticized view of Spanish architecture from the turn of the century. The walls outside were draped with thin veils of bougainvillea. Wide, white arches led to clean stairwells that introduced a visitor to the first and second floors. The apartment was clean and had a pretty light yellow tiled 1950's kitchen—something I later discovered to be "quintessentially Los Angeles." The single bedroom we shared was neither pretty nor quintessential.

My mother bought two squeaky foldout iron twin beds from Kmart. They sat side by side, parted by less than a foot, quietly screaming "internment camp." There would be no masturbating, no hugging my pillow and crying, no talking to myself, or writing in any sort of diary. Privacy simply became a problem I had to solve. Nearing sixteen, with my hormones raging, I had to figure out something that would give me both time to myself and stop the feelings that were pounding in the lower half of my torso. I came up with a genius but rather disgusting solution.

Back when I was eleven, my mom had given me my first enema in order to "purge the toxins." A girl we knew, the child actress Heather O'Rourke, had died from an undiagnosed bowel obstruction, and my mom had been put on high alert. You may recall Heather as the little girl in the film, *Poltergeist.* We knew her because her older sister, Tammy, and I had been in class at Danny Daniel's Dance Academy together and had both been cast in *Pennies from Heaven.* I didn't know Heather well. I just remember sitting at the farmers' market with her, a shy little girl, as we all ate pie, thinking she was eerily pale for a six-year-old. Other than that, she was as normal as any child could be—except she hadn't told her mother she wasn't pooping.

Because of what happened to Heather, being slightly constipated and not telling was now totally against my mother's

"Rules." If I didn't have a bowel movement every day, I had to confess, and that meant "the Bag."

"The Bag" was a strange ritual. I used a hot water bottle equipped with a hose and nozzle, hung it by a plastic hook on the towel rack, stuck the Vaseline-covered nozzle in my anus, and forced water up my colon until I couldn't stand it any longer. Then I would crawl desperately the toilet for a forced explosion of relief—it kind of felt like shooting a gun out my ass.

Although I hadn't done it very often before I was sixteen (because I hated it), I began experimenting with "The Bag" or "Bagging" as we began to call it, as a way to negotiate having private time away from my mother. Under the pretense of cleaning out my colon, I discovered I could sit in the bathroom for at least an hour and read a book, look at a magazine, or even listen to the radio. There, I could mostly avoid her endless intrusive chit-chat, "What are you doing? What are you reading? What are you thinking about? What is going on with you? What do you want to do for dinner?"

It wasn't that my mother was a stupid woman or always totally annoying—it was that she was trying to be my best friend. What exacerbated the situation was that we still couldn't afford to get me my own car. I was totally reliant on her to drive me around to school or auditions. To my chagrin, I often found I preferred the annoying conversations with my mother to those with the kids at school. It might have been "too much Mom all the time," but at least she thought about something other than sex, boys, and makeup.

In order to help myself to not think about sex, I became obsessed with PBS, also known as the Public Broadcasting Service. I often turned it on when I got home from school and kept it on until Mom finally slumped in the door after her new art and design class at Pasadena College. My mother had the idea she was going to become a graphic designer because design made more money than arts and crafts. She was determined to do something other than fall back on her legal skills. It seemed like a good idea at the time. I didn't mind that she wanted to be an artist—I just wished she wanted to be a mom who paid the bills and came home to be a mother to me—not the other way around.

When I hear stories about heroic parents who sacrifice everything to help their children have an education, while making sure their kids know "they can be absolutely anything they want to be when they grow up as long as they study hard," I must admit, I want to punch something and throw up. Lucky little shits.

In order to not think these thoughts and keep my mind on the end game, I turned my focus to the television for clues on how to be a better actor.

PBS in L.A. was an interesting mish-mash of American children's programming in the daytime and British Classics at night: *Masterpiece Theatre, Brideshead Revisited, I Claudius, Medea, Nickolas Nickelby, The Mystery Series, The Jewel in the Crown, Upstairs Downstairs*: these series contained some of the greatest actors from the Royal Shakespeare Company. Actors like Judi Dench, Derek Jacobi, Ian McKellen, and John Hurt (to name a few), gave me an alternate universe to project my aching, lonely, leered-at teenage body into—a passionate world of feeling, language, history, and story that strived to address the deepest of human emotions and concerns. Oh, how I longed to be in their world. I ached to feel a part of something important and not just another cog in another wheel headed tits first into oblivion.

Thus inspired, I signed up for some classes at Estelle Parsons Acting School, where I learned a few skills and a few facts. Skills like, "Acting is doing. What are you doing?" and facts like, "You have no skill at accents." I made friends with a nice young gay man, and my mom allowed us to go to a carnival together where we ate hot dogs and cotton candy. We paid for a ride where we sat on a swing high about the crowd while we were spun in a wide circle. Nervous about being out at night in a city I did not know, and dizzy and nauseated from the ride, I puked all over a very nice looking girl below.

"Sorry!" I said between heaves. "Sorry!"

She looked at me like I was the vomit.

I had hoped Los Angeles would be full of people like me—young actors that I would meet through work. I thought we would have adventures together, exploring the city. I had been hired for some good acting parts—four more episodes on *St. Elsewhere*, an episode of *Cheers*, and an ABC Afterschool Special about AIDS, but no real foundation had materialized.

L.A. felt to me like a place where everybody felt like nobody, so they pretended to be somebody until they didn't know who anybody really was at all.

"It's like there is a great big party going on somewhere and I haven't been invited," I confessed to Mom one afternoon on a drive to Fosters Freeze.

"But there is no party, Kate." My mother replied, "It's just all show. People here just love attention."

I knew one thing—I was not prepared to handle the attention that was to come as my breasts became more apparent. Older men in show business couldn't seem to stay away from me. I had to be careful or I would end up in a ditch—I knew that much. I was still a virgin and intended on staying that way a while longer. It took some effort.

In addition to the film director who auditioned me while feeling me up, there was also the TV producer who took me out to dinner to talk about "my future" while rubbing my leg under the table. And then there was the TV actor who took me to a quiet, private gym below the Paramount stage where we were working and danced me around to Paul Simon while he gently kissed my newly minted and glossed 16-year-old lips. He was the worst because, like my older high school crush, I thought he was in love with me, so I let my heart go a little. When someone on set pulled him aside and told him my age, he gave me the tape he played for me in the gym and disappeared.

I played that tape, *Graceland,* over and over for weeks afterwards, waiting for him to call, absolutely sure that he would. When he absolutely didn't, I felt absolutely nothing like Lolita.

In the album, Paul Simon sings, "Losing love is like a window in your heart. Everybody sees you're blown apart. Everybody feels the wind blow." But they don't.

"They take and take and they don't give anything, so what's the point?" I said to my mother in the car one day. "Men in L.A. are evil."

As I write this, I am sitting in a coffee shop, listening to some kid sit across from his dad talk about the courses he is

taking at school and how filmmaking is a more important class
for him to take than playwriting, blah blah blah. It is taking
every ounce of energy I have not to pick up my laptop computer
and whack him in the head with it. Oh my god. Now he is going
to talk about wanting to be an actor.

This kid's dad is clearly paying for every inch of his life:
his clothes, his food, and his education. He is sitting there
patiently listening to his son talk far too loudly for this tiny
coffee shop without a word of reprimand. I wonder if they have
any idea that I am dying inside. What I would have given for
a father who would have taken me to lunch, ask about what
classes I wanted to take, and pick up the check. What I would
have given.

My mother, circa 1987, was not listening to my rant about
men. This was all old news to her. We were driving home from
an audition, and she was pulling into her old standby, Fosters
Freeze.

"Waddaya want? Chocolate, vanilla, or strawberry?"

Mom loved her chocolate shake.

"I don't know," I said. I was disgusted with my life, and
ice cream wasn't going to fix that.

"Hey, you want to go to my art class with me on Sun-
days?"

Since moving to L.A., my mother had completely rebirthed
herself, dying to all of her obligations as a suburban tchotchke-
painting stage mother and emerging as a charcoal-covered
struggling painter of fine and graphic art. This class was full
of serious artists practicing the fine art of drawing the nude
figure.

"Hmm. I'll have a vanilla dip. Do you think they will mind?" I figured why not go to her class, as the only other option was staying home and masturbating, "bagging," or watching another round of *Star Trek*. "Do they have kids my age?"

Mom passed me a vanilla cone dipped in magic chocolate sauce that was supposed to harden in under a minute. "I don't think they will mind. You're old enough. HEY, FUCK YOU, ASSHOLE," she shouted out the window of the Mercedes, flipping the bird. "Goddamn prick! Almost side-swiped me!" She stuck her straw in her mouth, shifted gears, and sucked hard on her chocolate shake. Raising kids was hard enough. My mother didn't need a trucker up her ass.

When the weekend came, I begrudgingly went with Mom to her art class. I wasn't bad at repeating the shapes of the naked models on paper and didn't hate it as much as I thought I would. I was also starting to be impressed with how much talent my mom actually showed. I shook my head. "Who knew?" I thought. It began to dawn on me as I watched her draw that maybe she had put away her real dreams a long time ago, maybe even before she met my father. Those dreams had spilled out all over us—encompassing us in her frustrations. She gave my sister and me art supplies for Christmas, birthdays, and Easter, and took us to all the art stores and museums California had to offer. We learned to browse art history books and talk about color and light and composition while she browsed shade charts for tubes of paint for what felt like hours on end. It was an education, of sorts, in someone else's degree.

While I waited for her to finish drawing, I sipped a cup of coffee heavy with milk and sugar and began to daydream.

I imagined us in another town, where maybe we could run a donut shop and smoke pot and have wacky friends like in one of those sappy Hollywood movies. I thought how pretty my mom would be if she stopped cutting off all her hair and wearing those "fat people" clothes held up by elastic and snaps instead of a button. I imagined her getting a boyfriend who would stay over so I could have my own room. I imagined her as a hippie, a lawyer, a blonde housewife devoted to keeping her man—anything but an angry, repressed, depressed, fat and getting fatter ex-wife and resentful mother, insisting on living out her "bohemian artist" fantasy while her actress-daughter footed the bills.

I looked down the road at the role of provider that was slowly but surely becoming my fate and started to twitch. "I could run away and become a stripper," I thought. "I could run away and get hooked on drugs and not worry about taking care of anybody anymore. I could get skinny and fuck everybody in L.A., and then maybe somebody would take care of me because I gave such a good blowjob. Ha!"

I took a deep breath and contemplated this idea while I watched my mom elegantly sign her name to her sketch in cobalt blue charcoal.

"But then I would probably get raped and thrown off a bridge into the waterless L.A. River and no one would find my body for days until after seagulls had pecked my eyes out, and I was half-eaten by raccoons. Mom would have to come down and identify the remains of what was left of me, and she'd freak out completely and turn into a homeless woman wandering the streets of downtown, jabbering to herself about her lost stripper daughter who just wouldn't listen. Annie would never forgive me. She'd curse my soul for eternity in some ancient language, and then I'd have to live in some kind of tortured limbo hell forever and ever amen. So. Drug-addicted sex whore is probably not an option. Fuuuck."

As I swirled the coffee around the bottom of my cup, I thought about what else I could do.

"I'm not exactly a scholar. Who am I kidding? We can't afford for me to finish college, anyway. I can't type or spell. I have no skill that would make more than minimum wage at Orange Julius, and that sure as hell isn't going to pay the rent. So, there's really no choice. Fuck a goddamn duck. Acting it is. Goddamn it." I threw my cup in the trash. "Not having a choice really sucks the passion out of something," I thought.

After she finished her sketch and said goodbye to the teacher, Mom took me to lunch at a coffee shop nearby. Somehow she caught my vibe of frustration and decided to deal with it head on.

"Listen, Kate. I know this is hard on you. I can see it. But don't freak out, okay? I am going to get work eventually. Things are just tight right now. Your residuals are not coming in like I thought they would. So we're going to get some help, okay?"

I felt hope surge through me as Denny's all-day pancake special dropped on the table in front of me.

"WHAT?"

JOY!

Had she met a man? Had she broken down and called her father? Had Dad resurfaced? Had Donald Duck shown up on our doorstep with a Western Union Money Gram?

Seeing the look of hope in my eye, she quickly got to the point. "No, your father has not sent money or called or whatever it is you are thinking. He is an asshole; I thought that was clear. It has been pointed out to me that a lot of artists go to the welfare office and apply for money from the government until they start getting money from their work. So that is what we are going to do tomorrow morning, unless you have a better idea."

There it was—the dreaded lowest rung of the ladder. Welfare. There were no friends, no man, no job, nor family members coming to the rescue. My sister was sitting inside a fancy college, and my mom and I were going to line up for welfare.

How was this possible? I had given up everything. I had gone to every audition and every screen test; I had had dinner with awful older men who promised me work and gave me nothing but a slimy sloppy kiss on the mouth. I had literally whored myself out for this existence, and now we were going to the welfare office?

I was not amused.

"Don't get upset, Kate. I'm upset already. I don't need you making it worse. Pull yourself together. If you can't think of anything else, then don't complain."

I thought again about becoming a drug-addicted prostitute. "I could go be a stripper, Mom. What do you think? You know, dance around in my underwear, flash my tits? I hear that makes a shit load of dough, especially if you're a teenager." I was trying to be funny, but as soon as I said it, I wished I hadn't. A full-bore slap in the mouth came flying across the table and sent my Diet Coke spilling into my lap.

"Don't you ever. EVER. THINK ABOUT. THAT." She was not kidding in the least. "I'll call my father. I'll do something."

But she didn't call her father. The next morning we got up early, dressed silently, bought some donuts, and drove to the welfare office.

"Gonnah be oka-h, Kaht." The big chocolate cruller stuffed in her mouth like a sugary ball-gag made it hard to understand her words. "Gonnah be fah-n."

But it wasn't fine.

The welfare office was an old, ugly one-story building from the 1960's. Mousy florescent lights highlighted the dirt on the dingy, broken linoleum floors. Embarrassed men and women in shabby clothes stood in line with worn pieces of paper in their dry hands looking anywhere but at each other. It crossed my mind that this place might be a testament as to why people kill themselves. I was shocked at my mother's naïveté. What had she been thinking? That we would just sign up and they would hand out the money for free?

"No, mom. No," I leaned over to her where she sat in a faded orange plastic chair, whispering as quietly as I could. "Not like this."

I looked too young and shiny next to these people. She had to see it. I didn't want to be touched by their depressed energy or embarrass these people further by displaying my youth, my innocence—my potential opportunities versus their hopeless reality. Besides, it was too soon for me to admit defeat.

I pulled at her sweater. "Mom. C'mon. We can do better than this. I'll get a job soon. I won't leave you. Just please. Not this."

I could see she was having second thoughts. She too was shiny next to these unfortunate people—people who were desperate and frightened on a level even they didn't want to know about. She sat there for a moment longer in her loafers and khaki skirt, full of coffee and doughnuts, with a rich father and a generous mother she seemed to have so casually disowned and, I think, felt a little ashamed of herself.

"Okay, Kate. Okay. Let's go."

A few weeks and two-dozen cans of Campbell's soup for dinner later, the job came—a big theater job in New York. A workshop I had performed in earlier that year was going east for a pre-Broadway tryout in East Hampton, New York—full of hopes. I had done it. I had focused on changing our lives, and it had happened. It was the chance to get far away from heartless, theater-less, pants-less, coke-fueled, morally corrupted, desperate '80's L.A. In another town, we could try again to become different people, better people, or at least new people. I prayed this was the job and this was the town that would finally awaken a sense of responsibility in my mother and give me some freedom—freedom to figure out who the hell I really was.

"New York," I watched my mother roll the words around her mouth. "In New York, I could study at the Art Student's League. You could get yourself to auditions instead of me having to drive all over hell and gone. And Annie will only be a few miles away instead of across the country, so we could see her more often, right? Then we can all get an apartment together after she graduates."

Despite knowing that my sister would rather cut off her arm than move back in with us, I did not correct Mom's fantasy. I just knew that I needed to get out of L.A., or I was going to end up on the end of a dick or a needle or both.

I watched my mother's face carefully contemplate another move and tried to egg her along. "Change is good, right, Mom? New life? New chances? It's a good play. A good job for me."

Her face looked serious. She liked running away, but she had just started to really like her classes and her bohemian world. Moving to New York meant a big change—a change she wasn't sure she wanted and a big price tag to go with it. Theatre work was not going to supply endless amounts of residual checks like TV did. I watched her gaze at me—her now suddenly seventeen-year-old daughter who had given up her youth and her education and stayed loyal to her and her alone. I thought I saw a pang of maternal responsibility hit her square in the chest.

"I've got some money coming from my mother I didn't want to spend, but all right. Okay. Let's go."

Money

W e packed up the depressing iron beds, the foldout IKEA sofa, the art books, and the coffee maker, and put it all in a rented garage. Everything else went into suitcases that would take us from sunny California all the way to the East Coast, where our new life awaited. We checked the Mercedes for oil, bought maps of every state we planned on driving through, and a bag of oranges to remind us of home, of L.A. and the sweet promise it always held but rarely delivered. Thusly prepared for the great unknown, we hit the road.

Co-Captain of the USS Mercedes, I was to stay alert, work the radio, and watch the map—keeping my eyes on "the mother" to make sure she wasn't daydreaming and missing our next all-important exit. Mom had a vague idea of which states to drive through and could dictate from memory which highways were preferable. After all, she had taken this route many times in the era of mad dashes from Bill McClain—husband without a clue—but this made the drive like a ride down memory lane, and some of those memories made her hit the gas a little harder. I tried to remind her that this drive was going to be different. This drive was going to be one-way with no return.

"I remember when I first moved to California," she murmured along a long stretch of desert, "and when I drove over the mountains, the orange groves below exploded out for miles, the smell of oranges…was everywhere…and the color…the light…"

I didn't want to get lost in her memories. I focused on the desert, which I found quite soothing—the emptiness, quiet, and nothingness of it all. We drove as long as we could until exhaustion took over. I would then scour the map for some little hotel/motel nearby. These cheap hotels induced a feeling of dizzy indulgence. Everywhere we looked there were signs that we were wanted and special, and that our return to the same hotel chain would make the dancing neon bear outside do an extra hip-hop in his step.

Before bed we found a diner nearby—one that served gravy and mashed potatoes and a big slice of pie with ice cream—and then we drove "home" and watched TV until we were both too tired to keep our eyes open. In the morning, we looked forward to a hot shower, fresh towels, and the "Sunny Side Up Breakfast Deal." When it was time to move on, I watched my mother hand the lady behind the counter the card that would "charge it," and realized my new mantra.

I closed my eyes like a Buddhist Monk and whispered, "Moooooo-nnn-eeeeeeeeeey."

It was hard work to sit in the car for hours, but the comfort and familiarity of being in our reliable Mercedes gave us a pleasant feeling of being slightly above the world that passed outside. When the view stopped changing and began to dissolve into an endless valley of one strip mall after another, I would focus on the radio or some amorphous dream of becoming something other than nothing. Sometimes I would share these thoughts with my mom.

"For you to be nothing," stated Mom while chomping on a mouthful of orange, "is ridiculous and unacceptable. You are many things, my dear, but nothing is not one of them."

This would make me smile. Sometimes she truly did not suck.

At the edge of the Grand Canyon, we decided to splurge on a nicer hotel room and to stay an extra day. There was something in the air that needed to be shown respect and deference, something that felt like magic. Maybe it was just the splendor of the endlessly shifting color of the canyons baffling our eyes—nature, taking the stage front and center. It felt like it was the canyon's nature to be grand and beautiful. It knew no other way. I tried to take this wisdom inside me—pressing it into my heart.

"It is my nature," I whispered to myself at the edge of it all. "It is my nature to be grand."

We pulled the car over to a stretch of land. Mom threw her arms into the air and spun slowly around like Maria in *The Sound of Music* while I took her picture. To the passerby, I'm sure we made a funny duo—a big fat mama and her tiny, bespeckled teenage daughter. I often wondered what people who saw us thought. It was hard for me to consider that they might not have thought anything at all.

We passed town after town heavy with strip malls and fast food restaurants. Sometimes the only people outdoors were the ones hanging outside 7-11's or McDonald's—the disenfranchised embracing the franchise.

"See why I didn't want to go back to Illinois now?" Mom offered while tossing her free hand in the direction of the nothingness. "It's just all this. Nothing beautiful, just…this." She shook her head at the flatness of it all.

I thought twice about asking the next question but decided, "Screw it." I had a right to know the facts.

"What about your family? We see Grandma every few years, but we hardly ever see your dad. Don't you want to?" If we were going to be stuck for a few days more in the car, I figured we might as well get down to some conversation that went somewhere.

"No, Kate."

"Why not? " I held my breath and stared at the road. There was something different about her when she talked about her dad. She became younger and more vulnerable.

"He didn't want me around, my dear. Want to hear a story?"

"Yes."

"Well, here goes. You asked for it."

Had I?

"When I was twenty-two, my mother told me he was going to put me in a mental hospital. Do you know what they did in the 1950's to women in mental hospitals?"

"No."

"They put an ice pick in your brain. It's called a lobotomy. Remember that movie we saw about Francis Farmer? The actress?"

"Oh."

"Yeah. My mother didn't want me to turn into a vegetable, so she gave me two hundred dollars and the keys to the car and said, 'Go.' So I took the keys and I went. Got it?"

"I got it."

"Good. End of discussion."

And that was the end of any conversation of substance until we got within view of the New York City skyline.

With the help of a realtor, we soon found a cheap but safe studio apartment in an area called "Hell's Kitchen." The room was about eighteen feet long by fifteen feet wide, and we got to that space via a long hallway. I remember laughing about having to share a queen-sized foldout futon with my mother, even though I didn't really think it was that funny. I could see it meant a lot to her that I was going with the flow. It wasn't too hard. There was just something different happening in New York—something that smelled too good to not let myself laugh over our ridiculous situation.

Despite my years as a child actor fending off slobbering idiots, real "street savvy" hadn't come to me yet, and the streets of New York City were beginning to make it clear how desperately I needed it. The loud catcalls, whispers, and overt come-ons from construction workers were a big surprise. I privately wished it wasn't my equally clueless mother I was experiencing the city with, but some cool, knowledgeable, slightly older girlfriend who would say, "Sista, please. Pay no attention to those fools." I needed some pointers badly. I rationalized my lack of experience with the fact that I was probably more protected than any child my age. Once they saw her in action, no one in

New York would want to mess with my mother or her handful of keys.

Another security measure I discovered in this strange new neighborhood was my hair and skin. At that time, "Hell's Kitchen" was still territory belonging to the Irish mob, and my now red hair and pasty white skin seemed to act like a flag signaling I might be related to somebody formidable. I had heard a few stories about "The Westies" and their violent murders in the neighborhood, but I had never seen anything. It was hard to imagine they were as dangerous as the people on the news said. Not that a California girl knew what to look for. I only saw steely eyes watching from doorways—eyes that seemed to go back into nothingness. Those eyes could burn themselves into me, through me, on top of me. I wished one of them would just go crazy and fall in love with me. Grab me and take me away into one of those families with grandmothers that cook and fight and eat—families full of hard women that sit around the table telling outrageous stories—knitting and criticizing anyone outside the family. No one ever did. I like to think my mother had probably walked into one of the bars and made it clear no one was to touch her daughter, or she'd rip one of their Irish balls off and eat it for breakfast.

The play, which we had moved across the country for, was not the hit everyone had hoped it would be, nor the big money job my mother and I needed it to be. Instead it had become a painful introduction to the minute and intensely sensitive world of New York theatre. The original workshop production in Los Angeles had been fun. My role was small but important, and I gave it everything I had because everything was riding on it. The New York production was very different.

First of all, the other actresses in the all female cast were not the same as the ones in L.A. These ladies were older and tougher and more competitive than any I had ever encountered. They didn't know how hard life was for my mother and me. One of them in particular seemed to enjoy making my life hell. She didn't care that I was a West Coaster raised by a Midwesterner—raised to always be polite and nice and pretend to like somebody even if I didn't. She wanted me to step aside and let her take the stage. She complained about me to the producers, screamed at me in the actor house we all shared, and ignored me onstage. In order to stop the insanity, I moved into the house with the crew, crashing on the floor in a sleeping bag.

Honestly, I didn't know what it meant to be a "Mensch," or that we weren't supposed to say "good luck" before a show. I didn't realize I was mumbling my subtext or annoying other people pre-show with my vocal warm up. I also didn't have any idea that my age could be a threat to anyone. I felt like whatever efforts I made were just not good enough, neurotic enough, self-effacing enough, or funny enough.

"You GOT the part. Now show us WHY you got the part," proclaimed the director.

"What do you want me to do more of?" I asked, terrified I was going to get fired.

"WHAAAT? Darling, this is the THEA-TAH, not LOS ANGELES. You're going to have to SPEAK UP."

And there you had it.

Because I had been the only actor other than the star to be brought from the L.A. production, I had become the New

York punching bag, in that "Oh, she's from LOS ANGELES," condescending way that New York people can sometimes refer to those from the left coast.

I had the last laugh, at least. I was the only one with a positive review. I cut the article out of the paper and stared at it. "Cady McClain is especially appealing." No one had ever said anything nice about my acting before. Ever. I wasn't a natural actor and I knew it—my self-esteem was too far down the toilet—but this review would be posted on the board in the hallway. It was the greatest revenge I could think of.

At that moment I wondered if my father, who had been gone for five years without a word, would have been proud.

Just then, there was a knock at my dressing room door. I had been removing my stage makeup by covering my entire face with a heavy dose of Abolene Cream. The cream was thick but clear, like Vaseline, giving my face the look of a slightly smeared china doll.

The knock came again. With no time to wipe the cream off, I pushed the door open with my foot.

"Hello! Sorry! Hi, come in! Hi! Sorry!" I squinted through the greasy haze. "Just getting my makeup off!"

"Hi. It's Bob." He seemed to expect me to know who he was. I didn't.

"Hi, Bob! Come on in! I just gotta get this stuff off my face, ha ha. Can you give me a sec?"

"Bob Fosse."

I froze. I knew that name. That was a famous name. That was the guy who did that musical my mother owned the record of. The guy who did the choreography for the play we went to see in L.A called *Dancin'* that was really sexy and really good. He was a big-time dude, and he was standing there talking to me in my crappy little dressing room in the way back of the John Drew Theater with my face looking like something out of a dream sequence.

"OH! Hi, Bob! I, uh, um…I didn't know you were coming!" I frantically grabbed a towel and started wiping my hands like MacBeth's wife so that I could shake his without smearing it with greasy goop.

"You did a good job," he said, and with his giant old paw of a hand, ferociously strong, picked up my tiny half-child mitt and shook it. "Good work."

I was stunned into silence. This was a man—a grown man who had come to my play and praised my work generously as a fellow professional. This was the great Bob Fosse, legendary choreographer and director, praising me. But for a moment, he was also Dad—a dad who had come to see me in my play. In that moment, I loved him with the gratitude only a love-starved teenager can own. If he had asked me to do anything, I probably would have done it, if only he would just stay. I wondered if he could tell how I felt, if he could see the pain in my eyes and, maybe, if he too, needed to be needed. Perhaps he even needed it so badly that it had ruined every relationship he had been in. This moment held for one second more, and then he turned and walked out of the room.

I followed him out to the edge of my doorway and watched him walk down the hall toward an older red-headed woman who was talking animatedly with the other women in the show. She looked small and incredibly frail. When she turned toward us, I thought she looked slightly sad and a little scared of me. I didn't want her to be scared.

I called out, "Thank you, Bob! Thank you so much!"

Bob nodded with his back toward me and stepped next to the woman with the red hair, placing his hand on her back gently. I didn't understand why he looked guilty and slightly cowed, like he was indebted to the redhead for something. I also didn't understand why she didn't join him to say hi to me but just stared at me like a spooked cat. The only reason I could figure was that there must have been a bit of backstage theater being played out, a living theater with a long history that touched many, many lives and today touched with only the lightest breath, mine. Their magic was powerful.

That woman was Gwen Verdon: one of the greatest dancers ever known on Broadway and the long-suffering wife of the great dancer/director/choreographer and serial cheater, Bob Fosse.

After the play finished, things were quiet but had a new kind of deliciousness to them. I had been given "the nod" by a great man and felt encouraged.

"If Bob Fosse thought I was good, then goddamnit, maybe this acting thing could pan out for me after all," I thought to myself. Emboldened by that one small comment, I decided I was going to go for it. Acting could not only be how I paid the bills, but something that I could feel proud of making my own.

Since we didn't need a car in New York City, the Mercedes had been garaged, so I was free to travel to auditions in New York alone via the subway. On the subway, I would pretend that I was whoever I was auditioning to be. One time

I had to audition for the part of a Jewish Holocaust survivor. I put on a black wool skirt and sweater and put a kerchief over my hair. I didn't think for a minute that a "Shiksa" (Yiddish for a white, non-Jewish girl) should not be auditioning for such a part but thought maybe I could pull off being seen as Polish or Czech. Imagining this girl, who had survived with her family in tunnels underneath Berlin during WWII, I felt like a leaf that could have been blown away by a tiny gust. The horror of what the character had seen was too much. I sang her song and played my audition from this place—from this delicacy that I did not realize I could already relate to. It was a good audition from which I learned how acting could be both appearing in one world and disappearing from another.

The agent called that afternoon.

"They loved you. You did a great job, but they want a Jewish girl. Sorry."

It was nothing but it was something. Getting the part would have taken me on a different journey, and apparently what I needed to learn that day was something else—something for and about myself: I was pretty good at imagining. My New York agent recommended I study with a man named Michael Howard. Michael had studied at the Actor's Studio learning Lee Strasburg's "Method," but had broken off to explore other techniques. After a meeting with him, I became the youngest student he ever accepted into his master class. He didn't usually take students under the age of twenty-five. When he discovered my real age, he was shocked, but (I think) proud of my deception. Hours at the acting studio allowed me even more independence. Encouraged by my small victories, I decided the next step toward my getting a life of my own was to get my mother off my ass and into a job.

"Hey! Who is the mother and who is the child?" she hollered over a shared raisin bagel with cream cheese and coffee.

"I just think if you got a job here in the city, it would give us all some structure. I'm working. I'm trying to get work, anyway. Maybe you could just get a small, part-time job doing something, I don't know...maybe in art?" I would have said anything to get some income coming in and Mom going out.

"Jeez, Kate, you are such a killjoy sometimes!"

Miraculously, within a few weeks, she found a job she was willing to lower her standards to do. Maybe it was something about New York, or maybe it was seeing me actually grow up that made my mother want to start acting like an adult. I choose to believe she had a moment where she started to feel excited about the possibility of her own future. Such things can happen, even to a depressed, overweight, divorced forty-something-year-old.

Her first job in years would be at a famous art store on Canal Street called Pearl Paint. She was paid minimum wage to stand at a counter selling and organizing elegant pens. It wasn't brain surgery, but I was so proud I was speechless. I stood on the other side of the counter watching her on one leg with my other leg perched up like a flamingo, staring at her. Little fat mama was growing up.

"Oh for god's sake, WHAT?" my mother barked grouchily, looking oddly thinner and younger with a red store apron tied around her black turtleneck and blue fat lady pants. "For Christ's sake, Kate. Stop staring. I can work. I've always worked!"

I held in my smart-ass remarks and instead prayed homilies of thanks to the God that must exist if this was really happening.

I wondered again what had done it—what had changed her mind. Was it the sudden liberation from having to drive me all over hell and gone? Was it something about living in New York? Was she just feeling "kicky"? I couldn't figure it out, but I knew one thing—Annie had to be alerted. She would fall off her damn chair.

I went outside into the street, checked my change purse, and looked for the nearest payphone. Fortunately that day, my little purse was full of quarters, nickels, and dimes.

My sister Annie, after three years of undergraduate school, was now starting her Master's degree at an Ivy League school. A dizzying array of scholarships, loans, and a bit of sup- port from our grandfather held her future together one day at a time—all based on her grades.

A strange girl's voice answered at my sister's dorm. I could hear laughter bouncing up the hallway like red rubber balls, full of life. "Hello?"

"Can I speak to Annie McClain, please?"

"Annie?" she paused and yelled down the hall, "IS ANNIE HERE?" There was a pause and a rattle as she got back on the line. "Yeah, she's here. Who's calling?"

"It's her sister, Katie." I started counting the change in my purse.

"Okay. I think she's in the common room. Hang on a sec."

While I waited, I examined the pornographic graffiti on

the Canal Street public phone and the exotic street life around me. A Chinese man was rearranging his stand full of delicate paper carvings on the sidewalk to my right. I considered buying one and sending it to Annie, but then remembered she hated little paper crap.

"Hello?" Her voice was tight, like she was preparing to hear bad news.

"Annie!"

"Hi, Kate." She sounded tired. "Listen, I have to go to study hall. What is it? Mom okay?" Annie did not need another mama-drama or bad news.

"She got a job! Mom GOT A JOB!" I was sure my sister would faint dead away and waited for the thump of her body hitting the floor.

"Oh my god." There it was. "Oh. Shit. Wow." There was another long pause, during which I could feel my sister's whole being relax. Then I heard a chuckle. "Well, congratulations, huh? Tell her I said fucking congratulations."

"I will. Good luck up there."

"Thanks, Kate. Good luck to you, little mouse."

I decided to walk all the way from Canal Street to our tiny studio at 9th Avenue and 52nd Street. It was about forty blocks, but I didn't care. The blue sky seemed to stab through the buildings with a ferocious optimism that would not be denied.

"Mom has a job. Mom has a job. MOM has a JOB! WOW!"

Things were bound to get better now. I watched my feet march up the avenues and felt so proud of them. Their determination had taken Mom and me from a go-nowhere life in a city that ate its young to a do-something existence in a city where "if you could make it there, you could make it anywhere." As I passed by one shop after another—a hospital, a bank, a store with flags waving and bells hanging on strings tinkling "come in, come in"—I started to think other hopeful thoughts— thoughts about a grand and glorious future full of possibilities now that I was no longer the only member of the family who was bringing home the bacon.

I started to hum, and the hum began to take over, and as it did, I started to sing quietly to myself a little something I heard once on TV. No one noticed I was singing, and if they did, they didn't seem to care—there were too many people.

I have a knack for remembering lyrics, but not names or titles. Annie used to say I was a like a "subliminal jukebox," meaning a person knew what I was thinking by what I was singing.

This song got louder and louder as I humped it up Manhattan:

"If it's naughty to rouge your lips, shake your shoulders and shake your hips, let a lady confess, I wanna be bad…"

Sex and Death

I may have managed to keep my virginity intact until we got to New York, but by the time I was seventeen-going-on-eighteen, it was like a car alarm had gone off inside me. Construction workers howled at me like caged dogs, strangers tried to pick me up on the subway...even a street musician followed me down the sidewalk on his bike and demanded I kiss his cheek. My alarm was screaming, "Virgin here, get yer fresh, live virgin here!" in a city where everyone had practically screwed themselves to death.

"I have to get rid of this thing," I thought. "Or I'm going to get raped."

There was still no man at home to protect me—no authority to pronounce, "Our girl is going to go away to a good school with Decent People and getting away from these animals." Nope, it was just Mom: the protector who could not protect, just randomly attack without warning.

I told her about the street musician and the terror of being a virgin in a virgin-less world.

"I don't know how to handle it. It's like they know I

haven't had sex yet." I explained. "I try to be nice and stay out of trouble, but I had to beg that guy to not follow me down the street!"

My mother scrunched her brows together with a vaguely annoyed look and stared at me across a crowded futon. She was quiet for a long while. I thought she was terrified of her daughter's innocent power—terrified for me.

Finally she spoke. "Look, Kate, don't you worry about it. Everybody has sex sooner or later, okay? So will you. Meanwhile, don't talk to strangers. Don't even look at them."

It wasn't much, wasn't much at all, but it was the best she could do at that particular moment. Sorting pens at Pearl Paint was becoming more and more stressful, and she was beginning to have power struggles with her manager (again). She couldn't worry about me being harassed.

"Look, just promise me you won't be stupid. Don't let all this attention bother you now. Let it bother you when they <u>stop</u> paying attention. Trust me. It ends."

I suddenly saw something in my mother's face I hadn't before. It was a tiny tinge of jealousy and boy did it hurt—like a tiny slice of hate. This was unacceptable.

I decided then and there that if I got rid of my virginity, maybe I could kill two birds with one stone: my mom would stop hating me, and the men on the street would stop bothering me so much. It was a win-win situation. I just had to find somebody likeable enough to help me out. Love could be nowhere in the equation. No, no. Love would have to come later.

"There are so many guys in the world, Kate, just pick somebody," I thought one day over a regular coffee (milk and one sugar). "Just pick somebody and get it over with."

As I contemplated my options (acting class, stranger, street musician), I realized there was an interesting guy in my ballet class. He looked harmless and was funny. Besides, if he was straight, his pink tights proved he clearly was open-minded.

"Not much harm could be done by that one," I said to myself.

Besides, he wasn't like anybody I had ever met. He had short, curly blonde hair, a high voice, and a British accent. He was very pale, almost translucent. He also looked pretty good in his tights, which was hard to say about anyone, certainly a dude.

I had previously ignored him because it seemed to be against the rules to flirt in class. It was a serious dance establishment, after all. We were there to DANCE! DANCE! DANCE! However, if I was going to get rid of my "problem," I had to start giving him some encouragement. So I began to chat more while we waited for the class to begin, gently joking about our rather theatrical ballet teacher who was as round as an orange and clearly a screaming queen.

"'E's a friend of my pah-rents," said the Brit. "My folks ah in show bis-ness back home. Musicals. I'm just here for the summa."

"BINGO," I thought. "Per-fect-a-monga."

A few days later after class, I told him about my problem. He stared at me for a second, stunned. Then his face cracked into a half smile.

"Aren't you the funny one! Why certainly, dah-ling, it'll be my bloody pleasure!"

A few make-out sessions later (just for me to get warmed up), we went up to his apartment to get the deed done. He shared a tiny, three-room apartment in a furnished sublet on the Upper West Side with a couple of female dancers who were out for the day. His room contained little more than a foldout sofa. He gently pulled the ancient mattress from inside the cushions and smoothed the sheets for a more proper love nest.

"Do you want a drink or somethin', love?" He seemed a bit puzzled. I guess I didn't act like any other girls he had known. I hadn't wanted flowers, presents, or even a date.

"No thanks. I just want to get it over with."

"Well, ah-ren't you the romantic thing, then? All right, dear! Bottoms up! I'll get the rubber." And off went his tights.

His penis was much, much larger than I expected.

Why hadn't I thought of that? "Small me plus big him" might equal something really uncomfortable, but it was too late now. The rabbit was out of the bag. I'd just have to deal with it.

I lay down, pulling my own tights down around my ankles and closed my eyes, secretly wishing that I did love him and that it didn't have to be like this, or that there was somebody to tell me how to do it differently. I thought of the tennis player, the one who might have had real passion for me. What if I had let him put his penis inside me first? Maybe I'd still be at the beach, drinking margaritas and having barbecues.

"Ouch, ouch… ouch! OW!"

And that's how I had my cherry quickly and painfully popped.

"Well, there you ah, deah!" Ballet boy said cheerily, "You

ah officially not a virgin anymore!" He got up and circled the day in red on the calendar that hung on the door.

I felt bad for him. I didn't love him and this was something a person was supposed to do with someone that he or she loved. I felt like I should say something.

"Don't worry," I explained, "my mom won't be mad. I don't think she cares, really." Oh God, why did I say that? I knew she wouldn't care. She'd just be glad to see me down at the same level as herself.

"Right then. You want to stay here and rest? You're a bit bloody. Ear's a rag. I've got to run to class. Will I see you latah?"

"Yeah, sure."

"Good, then. Ta!"

I lay there with the rag between my legs and thought about my mom.

"Maybe she just expects me to be a whore," I thought. "Maybe because of what Dad did, she thinks I was made to be a whore." And I cried for a little while, believing that I might have been a tiny bit right.

The next day's confession to my mother was accompanied by coffee and a couple of chocolate-covered donuts, which were much thicker and greasier than the fluffy, light ones from California. She looked slightly annoyed at being asked to step up to her maternal responsibilities yet again.

"Well. Congratulations, huh? You are a woman now for sure. Okay. Hey, (munch munch), but, listen, babe, and I mean this," she took a dramatic pause and slurped up some milky coffee. "Whatever you are going to do, just don't be stupid about it, you know?" She leaned in so the people next to us at the counter wouldn't hear, "Don't worry about it. Don't feel bad, but don't be stupid, okay?"

This was not what I had imagined her saying.

"Jeez. Okay, okay!"

"No, Kate, listen (slurp, munch) I don't see you ever getting married, so don't worry about the men. Men are not important. Fuck if you must, but don't fall in love. It will ruin you. Look at me. Right? Love your work. Work is more important than a relationship, okay? If I have taught you anything, I hope you will remember that."

I looked at her like she had lost her mind.

"You don't ever see me getting married?"

My mom claimed to have psychic powers, so this was pretty bad news.

"Are you sure?"

"Look, Kate, seriously, don't bother me with this crap. I've got bigger things to worry about than this romance bullshit. Like I said, do what you want (munch). I don't care. Just don't forget: men are shits. And don't forget about your work."

I nodded my head and looked down at my donut. Another bit of beauty was being shot out of my heart, flying into the air like a tin can off a fence.

If work was all I could rely on and I was going to be an actress, then donuts would have to go. Donuts, boyfriends, marriage, babies, romance, roses, Daddy, sister, sweetness. According to Mom, it all had to go…deposited into a trash bag and taken to the chute to be dropped into the fire and not heard from again.

I saw women on the street in New York that looked like they had burned up long ago. They walked fast and sharp. I called them "The Shark Women of New York." They looked tough in their high heels, black suits, expensive haircuts, and red lipstick. I imagined they could probably club and eat a baby seal raw. I promised myself over and over that no matter what, no matter how hard life was, or how hard I had to be, I would never become like them.

"I will not be a shark woman. No matter what my mother says. I will hold onto something gentle about myself. I will continue to believe that someday Dad will come back for me. He will call and want me in his life. Annie will come back and things will be different. I must remember the dancing mice, my sister, and the pool. I must not get too tough."

But it was happening anyway. I could tell because I felt no love for the dancer. I had only slept with him to serve a private purpose.

I hated myself for that.

Three months later, I still hadn't got my period. I had seen an advertisement in Backstage (a show business newspaper) for an organization you could anonymously call to talk about your options if you were pregnant. I couldn't bring it up with my mother—not until I had a better idea of what I was dealing with. I didn't have a bump, but I danced five days a week and ate little more than yogurt and the occasional donut. I waited for Mom to leave the apartment and called Planned Parenthood.

The woman who answered asked me if I was planning on keeping the baby. When I said I didn't know, she said, "I feel sorry for you," and hung up on me.

This was confusing. I had thought Planned Parenthood was supposed to be a organization for women in conflict, but perhaps they weren't. Perhaps I had it wrong. Now I had to tell my mom.

"Goddamn self-righteous assholes. Shit!"

Mom was sitting in a squat-like position on the edge of the futon, which had now slid down off the sofa frame to the floor. She stared down between her feet.

"Jesus, Kate. What did I tell you," she mumbled quietly, her anger turning into something else.

"Maybe it's nothing."

She looked up at me—doubt all over her face. I remember thinking how sad she looked, like I had betrayed her somehow. My little breakout into the adult world was now costing her first steps as well—her art dreams potentially dashed again by the responsibility of another child. I couldn't stand it.

"Look, Ma. I don't know if I am pregnant. If I am, I don't know if I'm gonna want to keep it, okay? But I have to do something to find out, right? So, I think I need to go to a clinic, right? Find out for sure? Right? So, if I go to a clinic, will you come with me?" I had to take care of my mom now, or it was going to be back to the bottle, the tears, and the car all over again.

"Of course, don't be stupid." Despite her attitude, she was beginning to look like she was getting sucked into a memory—some journey in another dimension, half here, half somewhere not so pleasant.

"Mom? MOM."

"Yap. Mm huh. Okay then, Kate. Let's go. Let's get it over with. Help me find my shoes."

I found a clinic downtown that would give me a free sonogram and then talk to me about my options. All I had to do was show up, fill out a form, and wait my turn. After a ride downtown on the subway, we walked down the street where the clinic was located. Standing in front was a thin young woman in a gray coat holding a large placard that read, "ABORTION IS MURDER" on it. As soon as the girl saw us, she started screaming, "Do you want to kill your baby? It's MURDER! God will punish you for your sin!"

We couldn't move. It felt like the buildings of New York were growing up around us like giants stretching after a nap. Cars and dust started to swirl ever faster, reacting somehow to our lack of motion with more motion. The whole city seemed to say, "Fight! Fight! Fight!" My mom looked like she was going to either faint or snatch the poster and beat the girl to death with it. Grabbing her by the arm, I dragged Mom into the foyer of the building, bumping past the screaming girl. All I could manage was a loud, "EXCUSE ME!"

Inside the office, I sat down in a yellow plastic chair next to my ghostly pale mom. I grabbed a clipboard from the counter and started filling out a form. In between writing down my name and information, I stole glances at Mom. Her eyes looked glazed and watery, her mouth tight. It was winter, and the waiting area wasn't particularly well heated, so we both kept our big coats on. A small nurse with dark skin and a slight accent I couldn't figure out came over and took the form.

"Are chew Kah-tie Yo McCla-in?"

"Yes."

"Come with me, pleasth." She ushered me into the room, alone.

"I'll be right back, Ma. It'll be okay."

She nodded, still speechless.

The jelly on my stomach was cold, as was the machine, the paper gown, and the faces of the nurses who worked there. Everyone seemed tired. While the strangely accented woman rubbed a plastic wand over my stomach and looked for a fetus, I tried to imagine what it would be like to have a baby.

I was sure it would be a girl—a little girl full of sass, pigtails, and ribbons flying—who would call me "mommy" and hug me and want to protect me like I wanted to protect my mom. A little girl who liked frogs, wore rubber boots and dresses, sang at the top of her lungs, and banged pots and pans on the Fourth of July. A little girl who was everything I could not be, but who might be able to take me away from the only world I knew simply because of her needs. A real child—not an adult trying to forget she was ever young. She would simplify every decision from this point forward. I'd just have to keep her away from my mother.

"Mith. Mith Mc-Clain! Heylo!" The nurse was shouting at me, like I was underwater. "You'ah not pregnant. You prob-bly under some streth. That'th why you ah-ren't getting your per-i-od. Try to relath. Yoo know about condomth?"

"Oh, um, yes." I was a little disappointed and didn't want to hear "about condomth."

I mopped the gelatin off my tummy as the nurse helped me up off the table. Then it was back out into the waiting area, where she continued her speech whether I wanted to hear it or not.

"Well, we stroooongly suggesth yoo useth them. Thith ith wha-at they loo-ook like. Here is a pack to-oo take home with yo-ou. Ith that yo-r motha?"

My mom looked like she was going to explode into hysterical sobs if I was pregnant.

"Yep. That's her. Can I go now?"

"Yeth. Sign here-ah." The nurse turned to my mom. "You daughter ith fine. No problemth." Then off she went, presumably to find another young woman and her mother who needed straightening out.

As I stuffed the "condomths" in my purse, I noticed my mom was pulling ragged pieces of Kleenex out of her coat to stop the flood coming out her nose.

"Ma, you okay?" I asked, wondering how she managed to make absolutely everything about her.

Wiping her nose quickly, she stuffed the used Kleenex back into her pocket. "Yep. Fine. Let's go."

We did not discuss it any further but went to find some more hot coffee and donuts to take the edge off a rather challenging day.

A few weeks later, I booked another halfway decent job, this time an independent thriller called *Simple Justice*, (which I later titled "Simple Minded Justice") starring Cesar Romero and Doris Roberts. I was going to play the wife of the lead guy who gets pregnant and then put into a coma by being beaten up by robbers, which makes the lead guy go nuts. (You've seen this type of film one million times, I'm sure.) Anyway, the film was going to take me away for a few weeks to Pittsburgh to shoot, which was super exciting because I would be away from my mother as an adult for the first time ever.

A film, even if it was a schlocky one, was a big break for me. I was eighteen and knew if I came off well in the movie and the movie was successful, I'd stop having to audition and start "taking meetings." I'd be asked to ride in a town car at somebody else's expense to an incredibly expensive, super cool hotel, where I'd sit with a brilliant, yet eccentric director who was obsessed with me and wanted to make me the star of his multi-million dollar film. I didn't really care about being a movie star (I already knew it could come at a high price from watching Peter O'Toole) but knew there was a chance for me to get out of the underdog position of auditioning, and for that I would have given my left tit.

Auditioning sucks.

Anyway, while I was shooting this film, I was on a very strict diet. No fat, all salads, and steamed everything. I also worked out two hours a day no matter what. I was going to make the most of this opportunity if it killed me.

Then I got the phone call that changed everything.

"Hey Kate." It was my sister. Her voice sounded tired.

"Hey Anns, what's up?" I was happy she called. We had been talking less and less as she was sucked deeper and deeper into school.

She was blunt and to the point. "I'm with mom. We're in the hospital. She's fine but didn't want to worry you. She's having an operation. She's going to have both her breasts removed, so the cancer won't have a chance to spread. We know you are under a lot of pressure and didn't want to worry you. That's why we didn't tell you before. But she wants to talk to you before they take her in for the operation."

Cancer? Double mastectomy? WHAT?

Being protected from the truth felt like a slap in the face after all the honesty and harsh reality I had handled thus far. My eyes searched for a place to land—my breathing becoming quicker.

Annie put our mom on the phone. I listened to her usual jokes followed by lots of "don't worry's" and "I will be fine's." I wondered for a moment if maybe Annie had come home and made our mother take action, but that seemed impossible. Our mother did what she wanted when she wanted.

"It isn't fair to blame anyone or get mad," I told myself. "It's her body. Her life." I tried to think of her as some kind of warrior queen from the island of Lesbos—to shoot a straight arrow, off went one of the breasts, no question about it. This situation seemed to require losing both. I hadn't realized my mother was ambidextrous.

No more breasts. No more comfort. No more soft pillows for children to lean on.

After we hung up, I decided to give myself an enema. I needed to purge feelings of rage and helplessness. I ended up giving myself three. I figured I had to be thin, anyway, so who cared?

As the water shot out of me, making me double over with pain, my brain ran in circles. It was a movie, a real movie, and a real chance at making big money if it was successful. Maybe that's why they didn't tell me: they didn't want me to screw up my chance at doing well, didn't want to "disturb me," but god-damn if I wouldn't have liked to have been disturbed. Alone in the hotel bathroom, at least I could purge. Tears of anger ran down my face as my stomach cramped against the invasion and the oncoming explosion. Alone in the bathroom at least, it was clear who was in control.

The next day I lost all interest in making this film my big break. I had "had it" with pain and wanted relief. There were a few older men on the set who were paying me a lot of attention, men who up to that point I had dismissed in my decision to stay "professional" and "disciplined," but now they looked like an option for comfort. One fellow in particular drew my attention. He looked like a frog, but an interesting frog, with a matching, interesting froggie voice. I told the men I was just eighteen, but it didn't seem to make them want to be more cautious around me. In fact, it seemed to make them even hornier. Only froggie man played it cool, which I liked.

Eighteen. I can't stress enough how young that is. So many people like to think that sixteen is the "baby" part of teenage-dom, but let me tell you, eighteen is still a child. I shouldn't have been there alone. It wasn't the same as going to college where one is surrounded by kids his or her own age. These were adults playing very grown-up games. Part of me liked the attention, but another part was afraid of the adult men who seemed to goad each other on to worse and worse acts of language and debauchery in front of me, perhaps in the name of the "bad guys" they were playing, but I don't know. I don't buy that as an excuse. Some guys just egg each other on.

The shoot was coming to an end, and soon I knew I'd have

to go back to the horror of my breast-less mother. I decided I needed to forget it all for one night, and let some sort of normalcy wash over me, even if it meant I got hurt in the process.

"My mom doesn't respect me," I thought. "So why should I respect myself? Who cares? What does it matter if I sleep with some strange guy while making a film?"

So I went to Froggie's room and had something that resembled sex. I wanted to feel love but didn't feel anything but the pressure of his body against mine. It's hard to describe it. I had never been tossed around like a salad before. I thought back to my acting teacher who had said, "Always make mental notes of interesting feelings you have. You might want to use them later in a scene." I wasn't sure when I'd need the feeling of being lunch but made a note of it anyway.

When all was said and done, it was nice to be held. I liked feeling a body, the body of a man, bigger than me, strong and different—a man who could act like he might protect me—even if it was just for the night. I was degrading myself for this illusion of protection but didn't care. I needed to feel safe for a moment, even if it cost me my dignity. I could cut off that part of myself, cut it off with my inner axe, so a deeper part, the part that had to go home and see my mom's two-foot long scar, could be strong. It was a trade off but one that had to be made.

When I returned home from the shoot, Annie went back to school. We could barely look at much less speak to one another. A silent blame had grown up between us as if one of us could have done something to stop what happened but didn't. We had been so close to being free of our mother's control, so close to being able to be adults on our own in the world. Now we would be slaves to her pain, yet again, with our fear of abandonment high in our throats. There was no choice now. Nothing for my sister and I to do but ignore each other and proceed: put our heads down, get work, go to school, come home, and take care of our mom.

The Opera of Soap

Stability. I became obsessed with this word. A word that held out a promise of home, warmth, and the lost wonder of childhood. My mom couldn't be counted on to bring in money now because now that she was sick, it was all she could do to lift a brush and stroke her books of blank paper with one of hundreds of water colors she had hoarded in plastic tool boxes, bought on discount from Pearl Paint.

"You have to make money while you are young, Kate," my mother would say while propped up in bed with her art books. "When you are over 40, no one will want you anymore. So you have to do it now." It was a mantra I heard over and over.

I replied with what I thought was the only thing to say. "Don't worry, Mom. I'll get another job. I'll take care of you. I will always take care of you."

It was a call and response that became our relationship. The job at the art store was an anomaly. This was the reality. Dreams of the Royal Shakespeare Company and the theatre would have to wait. The theater needed actors that could tolerate the awkward discomfort that being regularly unemployed would inevitably produce and actors able to fight for roles that paid nothing but the respect of a small group of devotees. My mother's bottomless fear was not what the theater needed. If I was to have any life as an actor, any tiny little world where I could hold on to any amount of self-respect, I would have to suck it up and turn this life I was given into gold myself. In a moment of both revelation and self-sacrifice, I called my agents and said, "I need a steady job. I need a soap."

"Bend but do not break," I thought. "Bend but do not break."

Soap operas were well respected in New York because they were mostly cast with theater actors bulking up their income. It was a job that promised financial stability, emotional consistency, a schedule and (I imagined), a strong, supportive shoulder of like-minded actors to lean on while I took care of my mother.

My first soap opera screen test was for the role of Harley on *Guiding Light*. I thought I was well prepared, but when I stepped on set, I forgot all my lines. I remember the expression on the face of the young actor who was screen testing with me. He stared at me like I was about to faint, which I was. All I could focus on were the dust motes swirling in front of my eyes as the sweat trickled down my arms along the sides of my body. It took a booming voice coming from above saying, "That's all right, Cady. That's fine. Another time," to snap me out of it and realize I had completely blown it. I staggered off stage to find my mom waiting for me.

"How'd it go?" she had a worried look on her face. I must not have looked too confident.

"I lost it. I couldn't remember my lines. Not one." I wanted to bury my head under a rock.

I had an early audition for *All My Children* that had gone much better, but before I could go on a callback, I was booked on a TV series meant to focus on the actor Michael McKeon. A series was considered good money, so we were excited at the possibilities. Unfortunately, the pilot wasn't picked up and instead was released as a movie of the week called *A Father's Homecoming,* which I am sure no one will remember because it was just that forgettable. Some people told me I was good in it, but I still felt self-conscious and uptight, like I wasn't able to get out of my own way. Luckily for me, *All My Children* wasn't happy with the actress they hired for the role for which I had auditioned previously, and I was called back to audition again.

It turned out to be a role that would change my life—the role of "Dixie," a sweet but ambitious Southern belle who was manipulating as fast as she could in order to survive. Something about the role felt right to me. It wasn't just the fact I could relate to her hustling: it was her confidence and humor. Her character had a wonderful Southern humor, dry and sweet at the same time. She wasn't edgy or caustic like a New Yorker...she was charming. I didn't know anyone from the South but decided I liked them. I would get this part if it killed me.

First I had to meet again with the casting director, Joan D'Incecco. I think she could tell I was green but had something. This meeting got me in to meet with the producer, Steven Schenkle, a small Jewish man with gray hair and kind eyes. There was something about him I liked immediately. He wasn't a douche bag like my father or most men I met, for starters.

It was so strange to sit in a room across from his big desk and "act" like I was another person in another place while being judged by this kind stranger in a big leather swivel chair. Most rooms I auditioned in were moldy in a "cheap motel" sort of way. I looked around at the bookcases and nice rugs and thought, "So this is what money looks like," and I wanted it. I didn't care about any of the other actors in the waiting room or who I was matched up with to audition. I just wanted IN.

A few days later, the agents called and told me I had been chosen among a handful of other girls to screen test. This meant I was close to getting the part but not guaranteed anything. The agents would negotiate a contract first, and then I would do a final audition on camera to pass muster. If I got the part, then the deal would be set—no arguments. It didn't seem quite fair, but I have learned nothing in show business is fair—it's all just a matter of numbers. Five hundred people may be right for the part, but five thousand want it. If you want it more, you are going to have to prove it.

In preparation, I made a collage at home, filled with positive words, like "strength," "confidence," and "courage." I got tapes that helped me "affirm and envision" myself a "healthy and whole individual." I worked on my lines for the scene until I could say both mine and the other actor's, just in case. I willed myself to believe I could get this part—a part that held the promise of creating the one thing I wanted more than anything—stability.

When the day came for my screen test, I was nervous. I thought of my "inner axe" and kept it close. Whatever part of me started to freak out, I chopped it off and that was that.

Thoughts of "I can't..." were hacked off at the ankle and left to fall. Feelings of fear were beheaded. Anxiety attacked and amputated. I wore tons of deodorant just in case—there was no way I was going to let them see the sweat drip down my back as it did in my audition for *Guiding Light*.

On set, there was nothing more to do but throw myself into it.

"Listen to the director and do what he says. You must overcome your fear. You must," I said to myself over and over again.

And I did. For those few minutes when the camera rolled, time slowed down. I found myself in control, able to focus on the tiniest detail, able to move my eyebrow if I needed to or wanted to, without stopping the lines or slowing down the action of the scene. The lines came out like I wanted them to. I even kept a hold of the slight southern accent I was copying off of the movie *Coal Miner's Daughter* and closed the door on my exit without it hitting me on the ass. I was so proud.

The next day they called and offered me the part—a contract role with steady money for two years. Two years of no worrying about how to pay the bills or the next audition. All I had to do was keep the job, keep this wonderful, beautiful new chance at stability and a new life. Determined not to fail, I bought every positive thinking tape and every theater book I could find, and stayed in acting class so I could become better. I stretched on set, ate on set, even fell asleep on set once or twice. I was prepared to elevate myself to the highest level of acting that I knew existed—all to prove to the producers that I was worthy of their choice and should not be fired. The only problem was, the job was nothing like what I had spent count-less hours preparing for. NOTHING.

"What IS that smell?" I wondered.

After thirty years, the studio had managed to absorb some rather pungent orders. It smelled like old cum. I tried to touch as little as possible in my dressing room. The carpets looked like they needed to be burned in a secure area.

"Lysol," I thought. "Tomorrow, bring Lysol."

I was also horrified to learn the undeniable fact that on *All My Children* circa 1988, the acting was not as important as one's hair. After an hour in the makeup and hair room, mine discovered a volume it had never known. There were days I looked like something out of a Bon Jovi video.

Things didn't get much better in the wardrobe depart-ment. Since I was a new member of the cast, young and un-tested, I was on the bottom rung of the ladder. Therefore, I was given a lot of hand-me-downs from other characters. They weren't going to invest money in me until I proved myself. Somehow I managed to acquire all the costumes with enormous shoulder pads.

I tried to ignore the horror of my appearance and focus on learning my lines and rehearsing.

Rehearsal on soap operas is not like rehearsal in the the-atre. There is "blocking" with the director, followed by a brief conversation about the dialogue, followed by a few hours when you are supposed to get your hair and makeup done. If you want to spend more time working on your scene, you have to find your scene partner at an opportune moment and ask him or her to "run lines." This consists of actors saying the lines of the scene over and over again until someone can't take it anymore and begs for it to stop.

Most of the actors were very nice, but some of the "pros" (often called "vets") liked to give notes to their colleagues—something that is not considered cool in any other medium. Some of the best ones I got were along these lines: "Are you going to say it that way? Because I can't say my line right if you do," and "Give 'em tits and face. It's all about the camera, honey. Tits and face." That one was at least sort of useful. Then there were the notes from the actual directors.

"Do you LOVE him? Well, SHOW ME!" Meet legendary soap opera director Henry Kaplan. His notes to actors were unforgettable.

"You CALL THAT ACTING?" he would roar at us. "You are SEXY as a FISH."

If I had the nerve to speak up for myself he would reply with a curious smirk and the expression, "You are SOME PIECE of WORK!"

I knew he was kidding, or at least I thought he was, but there were days he left me in tears.

Every day I would memorize ten to thirty pages of dialogue, work hard to make some emotions that were "right" for the scene, and then flush it all away to get ready for the next series of scenes. Memorize, emote, and forget—five shows a week, fifty weeks a year. (We all got two weeks off at Christmas.) I knew I was lucky to have the job. It was great to work and even better to get the steady paycheck in the mail; however, after a while, the amount of dialogue and effort began to wear me down. Coming home to a sick mother was like having a second job. All the purging of food I was doing wasn't exactly helping, either. I started to feel faint.

Mom was not to be dissuaded from our newly found fortune. "It's always hard for those who are at the bottom of the ladder, Kate. In ten years, you will be rich doing the same thing, and it won't bother you anymore."

My new income afforded us a move to a larger apartment that cleverly masqueraded as a one bedroom. In pure New York-style, the landlord (in order to make a few extra bucks) had a wall built that divided the living room into two rooms—creating a tiny living room and a ridiculously small bedroom. We bought two cheap wooden twin bed frames from IKEA that fit in the room head to head—our feet wiggling at each other from inches away.

The apartment wasn't awful looking. Mom set up her easel in the living room and bought some small yellow finches. The birdcage sat in the window, and if they didn't mind the view of the parking lot, well, I couldn't complain. Mom liked it because it faced north, providing the "northern light" by which all artists (according to Mom) like to paint. There was an empty cat litter box under my mom's bed, which came into use when her back hurt so bad she couldn't get to the bathroom to pee. When she asked, I'd wake up in the middle of the night and help her straddle the cat box to urinate. Then I'd help her back into bed, taking the box to the bathroom to pour out the urine and wash it.

"Thank you, baby. Thank you. Get me my book, will you, dear?"

I won an Emmy in 1990 when we were living in that

apartment, only a year and a half into the job. It was a surreal moment for me. I felt so blessed by the group of actors I had the opportunity to work with—so grateful for their friendship, kindness, and support—I had to tell them all I loved them. Maybe it was a bit over the top, but I did love them for their warmth and acceptance of me—especially Michael E. Knight

Michael Knight, for those of you who bought this book and didn't watch All My Children, played my love interest on the show. His character was "Tad the Cad," a very naughty boy who slept with all the ladies.

When I first met Michael, I have to admit, he came off as arrogant. He would rewrite every scene until it was almost unrecognizable, forcing me to re-memorize all my dialogue. He was funny, however, and incredibly handsome, and because of his popularity with the viewers, he had gained a bit of carte blanche with the producers. Unfortunately, this only fueled his ego. I began to think there wasn't anyone on the planet as full of himself as he was. I also started to think that I liked him in a very big way. Try as I might to deny it, he had a magic that other men did not.

As the producers and writers discovered, we worked well together. We ended up spending countless hours rehearsing, rewriting, and talking about the script. He took me to lunch and invited me to group dinners. He bought me presents for my birthday—some crazy shoes he thought I'd like. He found out my shoe size just so he could get me the right ones. Eleven years my senior, he was a gentleman, a real one, and would not touch my younger self with a ten-foot pole. Besides, there was too much for us to lose by doing something as cliché as falling in love with each other in real life. For this, I blessed him, loved him, and hated him. I wanted so badly to feel something other than the weight of my mother's needs and endless responsibility. I didn't know what he felt but imagined he couldn't see me as anything but a sweet young actress whose mother would be all too happy to cut his balls off if he touched me—which wasn't too far from the truth.

"I guess I can love him on set," I thought, "When the cameras roll, I can completely and utterly love him there, and we can have that. He will think I am pretending and will never know how much I really love him—how grateful I am for him. I guess it's good enough, for now." But it wasn't. Every day was like being under a spell—a spell that he cast whenever he walked in the room. He was so funny, so full of humor laced with pain that I knew not everyone understood, but I did. That was one of our bonds. I ended up following him around, rubbing his shoulders on set, picking up his lunch from the guards at the front door when he couldn't—ever chaste, ever faithful.

After three years of working together, Michael left *All My Children* for a while to pursue bigger dreams, leaving me alone in a world I hadn't had to deal with because of our popularity as a couple on-screen. A dark world of insecurity among some of the actors and a tough attitude among some of the producers I hadn't realized existed.

One day when I was about to go on set, I went into the hair and makeup room to get a quick touch up. It was part of our job as actors—to not go on set looking messy. The only person in the room was a hairdresser that was known to work mostly on one actress. The rest of the beauty crew was on a break. I was supposed to be up on set in five minutes. I decided to say, "screw it" and jump in his chair for a minute so he could shellac some hairspray on me. A moment later, the actress who had claimed the hairdresser as her own walked in the room. She saw me getting touched up in "her" hairstylist's chair. I swear to God, she stopped, gasped dramatically with her hand over her heart, and walked out without saying more than, "Oh!" The hairdresser and I knew what "Oh!" meant, and it was not good. Then the phone rang.

"Uh huh. Yes. Mmm. Okay. Yes, I see. Okay."

This particular hairdresser was a bit flamboyant. He had a penchant for exhaling heavily through his nose when under stress and managed the pressure by a savvy yet destructive combination of nips of vodka from the supply closet and frequent trips to the loading dock for a heavy smoke.

A show was about to begin.

"How do you feel," he gently offered, "about a change?" The nasal exhortations began.

I said, "Oh, no."

He began to comb my hair under, rolling it up so it became more like a bob and clipping it in place. "I think (snort, whoosh) you'd look really good (whoosh, snort) with short hair, don't you?"

He stopped and made a little, "Hmm?" expression, presenting his creation to me with one comb sticking out of his hand like a magician's wand and the other firmly planted in my head.

I wanted to vomit. All I had done was allow him to brush my hair before I went on set. I was a pudgy blonde with a big nose, no threat to the actress who had been on the show for years already.

"Can you excuse me for a second?"

"Sure, sure," he sighed, deep with relief. My leaving his chair was best for his future career with what's-her-name. I went straight to my dressing room and called the executive producer at the time.

"I am so sorry to bother you but..." I explained what had just happened. "I mean, if it looks like a fish and walks like a fish, it's a fish, right?"

"Yep. It's a fish, Cady. Don't worry. I will take care of it. Let's talk tomorrow." This was a straight up, no-nonsense woman. I felt sure she would understand that I wasn't a threat to anyone. I wasn't that competitive. I just did my job, went home, and tried not to embarrass myself. Apparently, it didn't matter what I did or didn't do. I was in "her" chair, and unbeknownst to me, that was a declaration of war.

The next day I was called down to the head office.

"We've decided that we would like you to have a new look. We want you to cut your hair short after all."

Ever dutiful, I went to a very nice salon on the East side of Manhattan and came back with a short, but (I thought) still charming haircut. I thought I had done my best to be a team player. I thought there was no way I could be a threat any longer. I did it. I cut it. Game over. We could hardly look any less alike. I thought wrong. The phone in my dressing room rang. It was the executive producer again.

"We'd like to send you to her (the actress') hairdresser," she said.

I shook my head. This was not good. Now I was going to be taught a lesson.

I truly had no choice. I had a mother with cancer to provide for. My motivation was, no matter what people thought of me, to make sure I survived the job. So off to the new hairdresser I went.

His first words told me everything. "Are you ready for a change?"

I shrugged. "I guess so. They sent me here. My hair is already short. I don't know what they want."

"Okay! Here we go!" He said, throwing a cape around me like Houdini. Within five minutes, he promptly cut off ALL of my hair. Dachau short. Mia Farrow in *Rosemary's Baby* short. Then they sent me to a makeup artist who plucked my eyebrows until they were a thin line. I had to admit that with the cape around my neck, it was rather "high fashion." It was when they took the cape off and I was revealed NOT to be a hundred pound soaking wet five-foot-eleven model, but a hundred-and-twenty-pound, five-foot-two, tiny actress, that suddenly they realized it was wrong. In fact I looked like a horse with its mane cut off. And that is exactly what I was.

When I showed up on set the next day, the producer called the hair room in a panic, asking them, "What did she do?"

Years later, I found out everyone had thought the whole thing had been my idea.

From that point onward, long hair felt dangerous, like a flag asking for attack. Long hair had brought me bad attention from those who found youth something to be dominated, crushed, or owned. I began cutting my hair anxiously, impulsively—desperately trying to destroy or reinvent myself in some form that wouldn't upset people. I hammered away at my physical identity as if I could change my circumstances by changing my outsides. I guess it was "experimenting," sort of, but actors under a TV contract aren't really allowed those kinds of processes. Actors working on TV are supposed to stay the same or at least be who the audience and producers want them to be, which on a soap is usually beautiful.

After four years, I was exhausted. I had saved a fair amount of money—enough to buy some time away from acting, or so I thought. Despite having all my hair hacked off, winning the Emmy made me feel like perhaps I was really the artist I had dreamed of becoming, and if I was, that maybe I could try doing other types of projects. It seemed feasible. My agent wanted me to leave the soap. He thought I had a great career ahead of me. My mother's cancer had been nipped in the bud with chemo, and she seemed happy to be back up again, toddling around Hell's Kitchen, sampling the international kitchens and doodling in her art books. I thought perhaps I could even try going to college like other kids my age.

Thus began *The Drama at Lunch*.

ME: I think I should quit the soap.

MOM: (big sigh)

ME: I'm exhausted.

MOM: (with irritated look) I'm dying.

ME: You're better now. Look, I'll make money doing something else.

MOM: Why don't you buy a house? Then you will have money saved and later you can quit and do something else.

ME: A HOUSE?!

MOM: Okay then. Just get me through my death, and then you can quit.

ME: Oh my God.

What I heard later after mom had a couple drinks:

MOM (screaming and wringing her hands): "You are so selfish. I don't know why I try anymore. I'm dying. You are just like your alcoholic asshole of a father!"

After a few more tries to negotiate some emotional treaty that would allow me a fraction more of my own life, I decided I would rather cut off my head and put it in the refrigerator than try to tell my mother "No."

Breakdown, Breakthrough

All the fun-filled drama at home and work left me little time to investigate the youthful, playful side of my adopted hometown. My god, I was living in New York City, self-prescribed center of the universe! Where nightclubs and faceless liaisons were a sexy calling card to give you entrée to a better party, where just walking the streets made you feel like a midnight cowboy. New York: home of naked, shit-covered performance art, CBGB's rock and roll geeks, drugs I never heard of, and freezing SOHO artists lighting bonfires and making jazz in abandoned factory lofts. The poets, prophets, and perverts of the east, west, and central village, the untamed gays of Chelsea, the madness of downtown money, the wealth and culture beyond imagination of the Upper East Side made this place the hairy navel of the world. A big, red, worm-ridden, half-poisoned, half-blessed magic Big Apple!

Sadly, all of this was happening around me, but not to me. I worked. I went home. I walked around the block. Worked. Shit. Went home. I realized the only way I was going to have a little bit of fun was to move my mother out somehow, pay for it, then find and pay for my own apartment, some little room where my mother couldn't open the door and suddenly dominate every square inch. A place where I could have a lover or not take a shit or not, sit in peace and smoke cigarettes...or not.

The idea came to me from one of Annie's genius turns of phrases. During a rare discussion about what to do with Mom, she had said, "It's too bad we can't just farm her out."

"Farm her out," I thought, "YES. Put her into a field far away, where she can graze on the grass to her heart's content."

I thought it was too pretty a carrot for my mom to resist, so I went for it, pouring her a nice strong drink.

"Hey, Mom, how would you like it if I stayed on the soap and we rented a house in the country?" Stirring the glass of vodka and lime, I bolstered myself into the ruse. "Someplace near a farm, maybe? We could have a real home there. I could just get some little studio in the city for the long work days, but I would come home all the time, weekends, you know? And Annie could come home more then too since we'll have more room. What do you think?"

I was breathless and terrified. Another round of guilt trips and "You don't love me's" coming out of my mom would have pushed me into becoming a gutter drunk. I watched her picturing it in her mind as she slurped her vodka tonic. She could stay "Mom" and play house all day; I would continue to play "Dad" and make the money, riding home on the train on weekends and short days; and Annie could play "daughter and best friend," coming home from school on breaks to her own room. All of us would still be together. It was everything she wanted.

"What a wonderful idea, Kate. Shall we go look at houses

this weekend?"

After a few trips on the Metro-North railway up the Long Island Sound to Connecticut and some trolling around the better doorman buildings near where the soap was shot, our new properties were quickly decided on: a white, 1950's Cape Cod-style three-bedroom house with a view of a pond for the family, and a tiny jewel box studio in a Beaux Arts building on the Upper West side with a slice of a view of the Hudson River for me. I smiled and tried not to barf as I wrote the rent checks—nine hundred for the apartment, two thousand for the house, plus security deposits. I told myself it was not only another step forward, but that maybe we would be okay again if were all together in a house—a real house like a real family, instead of endlessly chasing survival.

The house in Connecticut oozed charm. Every room had a feeling of faded 50's elegance to it. There was even a "study" with a built-in bar, wood paneling, and bookshelves. Compared to the tiny, stained condominiums and apartments we had been squeaking by in for the last ten years, this was nirvana. The living room was so huge we decided to get out all the old furniture Mom had squirreled away in storage.

Sitting by the fireplace in a house—a respectable house in a respectable location—I suddenly wept with gratitude. I couldn't think anymore about the pain I felt about being the breadwinner being the breadwinner at twenty-two years old. I only thought about how wonderful it was for us to no longer be living in a temporary shithole.

"I'll need to do a little shopping, Kate, to make this place work," Mom announced once she woke up and discovered the consignment stores littering the area. Boy, did she. I almost didn't mind. It made her happy. She bought curtains that matched the bedspreads, new rugs and towels, a grand dining table with eight matching chairs and a sideboard, a carved chest for the living room and new rugs for the bedrooms, new dishes, new glasses, new pillows and throws, new accent pieces...I just handed over my money and let her do as she pleased.

Even I loved going to Williams Sonoma and bringing home ridiculous contraptions: a juicer, a toaster oven, a new blender, a brew-in-one coffee grinder and coffee maker, kitchen towels with the name "Williams Sonoma" woven into them. I loved all of it. For all of the pain that it caused me, the soap money began to buy the things that said, "HOME. SAFE. SECURE."

While I collected kitchenware, my mom was shedding her bohemian self and adopting a new one: "The East Coast country mother of a (yes, that's my daughter) Soap Opera Star." She dressed in tweeds and silk scarves held together by replication broaches from the Metropolitan Museum of Art, bought us all classic trench coats from "London Fog," monogrammed silk bags for our pantyhose and underwear, and silver cigarette holders with matching lighters.

"If you are going to develop a nasty habit, Kate," she pronounced about my smoking, slapping the lighter on the coffee table, "for God's sake, do it like a lady."

Off the kitchen she created an office for herself where she could handle the bills and my fan mail, paying herself a handsome thirty thousand a year for her services.

"See, I've got a job! I'm working for you now, Kate!" she

spouted sarcastically.

I put up and shut up because for once in my life, I could always leave.

My mom had only agreed to let me have a studio apartment on the Upper West Side because it was close to my job—the fountain from which all good things sprang. If I had only been a thirty-something married man with two kids, having a house in the country and an apartment in the city might have been a dream come true, but these circumstances did not exactly reflect the youthful buoyancy and liberation that I had hoped the apartment would provide.

First of all, the Upper West Side was so clean, so boring, so...white. Old white people, mostly, stood outside of their turn-of-the-century brownstones stuffed to the gills with newspapers and crap, like birds on a beach looking left, looking right, looking left.

In my new apartment I could at least comfort my newly discovered loneliness with beauty. Molded ceilings and hand-cut wooden floors made way for large windows with Juliet balconies. Together my mom and I painted the walls light yellow and hung filmy curtains that blew into the room in soft, curved shapes. Shopping made my mother so happy it was hard not to acquiesce to her whims on how to furnish it. I had just wanted a big, white, foldout sofa, like in some '80's fantasy movie, but she wouldn't hear of it. I had to have something better now that I had acquiesced to my role as "bread-winner" and a space that would reflect the part.

With money from the soap that might have bought a college education, my mom encouraged me to buy an 18th century

French baroque bed and matching bureau, oriental rugs with a classical roman-style motif, and red velvet chairs with carved wooden frames. We decorated the walls with ornately framed soap magazine articles (featuring me), and antique pictures of actors in theatrical poses. We bought dried flowers in silver pots, thick, plush red towels, and matching cheap beaux-arts dishware, while packing the half-sized refrigerator with red wine and non-fat foods. I wished my mother would back off the spending, but I couldn't have cheap furniture now and buy something better in later life. Later life was when I would become a "nobody with nothing."

"Look! You will always have nice furniture now!" she cried, triumphant over my purchase of a giant French dish cabinet.

I knew I was lucky to live so grandly, but it made me feel like I was living in a museum. I felt like a faceless, voiceless mannequin standing in one of the Metropolitan Museum of Art rooms, looking out and screaming "What am I DOING in here? I'm twenty-two, not forty-two!" Constantly pulled between the desire to take care of and appease my dying mother and the desire to figure out who I was and have some kind of life of my own, I comforted my angst with pints of Haagen-Dazs ice cream, Billie Holiday recordings, bottles of red wine, and laxatives.

I wasn't to be left in my drama for long. The cancer had come back in a small lump in her neck, which would require radiation treatments, the doctors said, painful but doable.

Her death imminent, the idea that she might die without me knowing who she truly was finally drove me to confront her. I took a train from the city up to the house, where she was recovering from her latest treatment. I needed to know every-thing—why her father wanted to give her a lobotomy, why she refused to ask him for money, and why she never let her family into her private life. She didn't like me pressing.

"Ma, what's the story with your family? Why don't we see them? Did something happen when you were a kid? If you are going to die on me, I think it's only fair you tell me."

"Aw, crap, Kate. Now? Really?"

"Really. It's time. I need to know."

"Ah Christ. All right. Don't say I didn't warn you."

My mom told me she had come of age in the 1950's. She had all the accoutrements of her generation: bobby socks and a-line skirts, roller skating parties, cotillions, and a Catholic girls' school. She had a hardworking, rich enough father and a stay-at-home mother ensconced in a large white Cape Cod house in the suburbs of Illinois. There were green lawns to play on in summer, skiing in winter, and large family gatherings throughout the year. In the grand scheme of things, there was nothing she wanted for, nothing except attention. Unfortunate-ly, she didn't get the kind she wanted.

She told me that when she was five years old, a little boy that lived next door had taken her to the backyard and asked her if she wanted to see his electric pencil. She said yes and he took out his penis. He told her to touch it and she did.

When she went home, she told her parents what had hap-pened. Her mom refused to believe her and her dad was very angry. He decided if it had actually happened, then it must have been her fault. So he took her to the bathroom and beat her on her small, warm, naked child's bottom. He bent her over the bathtub and beat her hard with a leather belt, which sometimes smarted between her legs, sometimes hitting her there with the buckle. She said this happened more than once.

As she grew into her teens, she became a rebel, resisting any authority. She couldn't wait to move to college in New York, where she hoped to become a fashion designer. But New York didn't turn out so well, for reasons she wouldn't say. She came home to go to a local school, and while there, a fellow student broke into her dorm room. He crawled through the window and raped her. Afterwards, he told her she had made him do it. She told no one, but after a few months, she realized she was pregnant.

"Oh my god! Did you go to the authorities? Did he go to jail?" I was dumbfounded by her story.

"No, Kate. It was different then. They thought it was my fault." Her voice was flat and calm.

"What?"

"It was the '50's, Kate. Women didn't have a fucking leg to stand on."

Abortion was not legal in Illinois in the 1950's, or anywhere for that matter. At twenty-one years old, she was not willing to face the illegal slaughterhouses where women could risk death to be free of an unwanted pregnancy. Instead, her parents scuttled her away to a special "Home for Wayward Girls," where she was forced to sit out the pregnancy around a bunch of well meaning but humorless nuns. It was when she returned home that she learned about her father's plans to give her a lobotomy. That's when her mother gave her two hundred dollars and the keys to the car and told her to go far away for a long time, which she did.

"What was it?" I asked.

"What was what?"

"The baby. Was it a boy or a girl?"

She sighed. "A boy."

"What was his name?"

Her voice got softer. "I don't know."

"Did you ever see him again?"

"No."

"Where would he be? Illinois?"

"Probably."

"Do you want me to find him?"

"No."

"Don't you think he may want to know who his real mom is? I would."

"Kate."

"You really don't know his name? I mean…he's my brother."

"I guess you could find it."

"You never wanted to find him?"

"No, Kate. No. I didn't. Now please, let's leave it." She took a big sigh. "God, you're a pushy child."

A Man, a MasterCard, and a Muffin

fter returning home from that weekend, I couldn't stop thinking about the brother I had out there, somewhere. I recalled my mom telling me when I was little that if I was a boy, I was going to be named "Andrew" and wondered if that was his name. I felt so bad for him. I prayed. I wrote in journal after journal. Should I have been a boy? Had she really wanted me? Should I have been born? Did I only exist to take care of her? I started to consider ways to kill myself. I did not understand why I felt the way I did.

I did know sex was the one experience Mom wouldn't try to control. For some reason, the Queen of Lesbos didn't have a leg to stand on when it came to my sex life. Maybe it was her rape, her lost child, the donation of her breasts to the AMA, or her disappointing marriage that conspired to suck all the passion for men out of her, but my mom tended to get very quiet when it came to my sex life.

"Men can be good," I told my mother in my mind. "I will let a man touch me and maybe it will hurt, and maybe I will get pregnant, and maybe it will even break my heart, but there is nothing you can do to stop it. I've had it with the bitterness, the loathing, the sickness, loss, and death. Not all men are bad, Ma."

Her voice was now within me, hitting below the belt. It said, "Just don't get pregnant, Kate. Do yourself a favor."

I hate to admit it but at that age, I wasn't very picky when it came to sexual partners. It didn't matter what guys looked like, what they wore, or even what they did for a living. It only mattered if they had more freedom than I did. I found it more attractive on men than money, good looks, talent, or even sexual ability. Their liberation was my life affirmation, canceling out all the moments of my mother's dying, the smell of chemo and shit, the challenge of the checkbook, the horror of the past, the lost father, and the cage of responsibility I had found myself trapped in like a rat.

I succumbed to my first affair with an older man when I was twenty-two. Some might say I was looking for a father, but it was more than that. I needed nothing less than a monster poet to aggravate and challenge me—to divide me from the sanitizing effect of corporate entertainment and the smell of death—an intelligent bastard who would cover me in his filthy creativity and intellect, cleansing me in succulent decadence. No less would do.

I discovered it in Curt.

Curt Dempster was the teacher of my directing class— and the creative director of a theater company called Ensemble Studio Theater (EST). Our relationship was an education into a world of freedom and artistry I desperately idealized: a world of art, sacrifice, and intellect. Did he break my heart? Perhaps a little, but only because he was true to himself and would not be owned. Silly me, I wanted him to be my full-time boyfriend.

Curt's art and sacrifice were obvious: his company, although deeply respected in the business of show for its one-act plays and gritty performances, seemed to be eternally broke. Despite Curt's lack of ability to make money, he helped nurture the voices of such diverse and important theater talents as Wendy Wasserstein, John Patrick Shanley, Christopher Durang, David Mamet, and Horton Foote. He was clearly helping create greatness. What I called his bullshit went along these lines: "If you make money from it, it isn't art." I just didn't get it. I understood the purists and their intent to be free and make something beautiful just for its own sake, but to call something brilliant "not art" because the creator decided to hustle it/sell it/publicize it so he/she could pay his/her rent, better his/her circumstances? I realized what he was trying to say—that art could only be made freely when one doesn't have to consider the financial ramifications—but it did make me feel dirty as a struggling actor with high ideals who was also deeply in touch with how much being poor sucked.

I was twenty-two and Curt was fifty when we began our affair. While I was in my petite palace, he was living in the same cheap, first floor, studio apartment he had moved into as a young man. He had almost no possessions—a twin bed, some books, and a few small paintings. I knew he loved his work, but I wondered why he was with me. He was a genius. He did watch *All My Children* one time at my request and told me, "You're all alone up there." I couldn't say I agreed, but I appreciated the faith, never forgetting the comment. It did help me realize that even though I threw every bit of my energy and artistry into the scenes I acted on the soap, took classes, and did plays on the side, the "show-a-day" mentality of soap operas was an endless sponge sucking up whatever I had to give—a factory with no beginning and no end, squeezing out dollars. I liked dollars, but I also wanted to be an artist.

In his class he would say oddball things like, "Flap your flips," which meant, "Get up there and do something interesting. Don't take yourself too seriously, but do it." Or, "Keep your eye upon the donut, not upon the hole." He didn't put acting or directing on a pedestal. He was funny, brilliant, and afraid of no one, least of all me.

Looking back, I realize he was the model of the kind of man I would seek out again and again—smart, funny, independent, rebellious, somewhat distant, and seemingly unafraid. Now, I think below the surface of his confidence, ambition, and obvious talent, something tortured him terribly. Something that ended up torturing everyone else, especially anyone who loved him. I've spent a fair amount of time trying to understand this dynamic, this "brilliant/funny man who protects himself from the world." It is a personality I have seen in so many of the men I have known and loved, men who were clearly more talented variations of my father. I think it has to do with their ambition for themselves, the world's reaction to that, and their inability to reckon the differences between the two. The world is not always kind to talent combined with brutal honesty. "Too much truth" is like too much booze: it makes our humanity look sloppy and random, and most people don't like to look in that mirror. Most people generally like a cleaned-up "show of effort" followed by a distinctly happy ending.

After about a year, when I found out he was enjoying more pastures than mine, I had to call it quits. I may have been screwed up, but I really didn't want to be "old what's her name." Oddly enough, I heard he had a child with the woman he was dating while he was seeing me. I wonder at times if he drove her crazy with his independence or if she was just different than me—more tolerant, more bohemian, more able to handle the long leash he needed to feel free. All I knew at that moment was I did not have the courage to be poor for my art.

Thirteen years after our little dalliance, I heard something very sad. It was a snowy morning in January 2007, and I was riding in the back seat of a black Lincoln Town car on my way to the As the World Turns studios in Brooklyn. An actress that I was sharing a ride with casually mentioned what she had just heard: that the famous Curt Dempster had hung himself in his West Village apartment. She didn't know that I knew him. It was just the news of the day. Apparently, he was found quickly, but if it wasn't for his two dogs barking up a storm, he could have hung there for god knows how long. It was horrible to think of this huge, powerful, brilliant man hanging by his neck from a rope. It hit me hard and suddenly, lodging in my throat. I didn't want my friend to see me like that—exposed as a girl who had once loved—inappropriately and foolishly—a man old enough to be her father. She did notice, however, and I quickly made up a story full of half-truths. I studied with him...he was a great teacher, etc. I didn't think she could understand how I could have appreciated being in the arms of what I considered a great artist. Naïve ambition is often misunderstood. It is

thought of as something obscene, instead of a strife unique to the
young—a tender and wild longing to be full, mature, exquisite,
unique, adored, and actualized, and a willingness to take great
risks in order to be so.

After years of contemplation, I decided there was some-
thing almost beautiful about the way he had chosen to die. It
was completely truthful to who he was—at least the man I had
known. That man wasn't the kind of person who liked to be
trapped by anything, much less what I heard was a deteriorat-
ing mind being forced to fundraise for his company. The evil he
had decried—selling art for money—had come calling for his
soul and he refused it. Rich people wanted to recognize him, but
they also wanted "dinner and a show" for their dollar: a court-
ing replete with a glimpse into the inner workings of the artistic
process. I don't blame them; it's just a fact. The man I knew
hated glad-handing, thanking people, and what he might have
called "obsequious ass kissing." He was no ringleader: he was
an artistic director—guiding the souls of writers. I believe that
to Curt, being lowered to the role of fundraising was the epitome
of being the theater world's bitch. He was too proud, too cre-
ative, too free for that kind of glad-handing. He didn't aspire to
be a doddering old fool, like some people do, sucking the milk of
kindness off others while they loom and titter behind his back.
I say it was his choice, his life. We can call it selfish because it
affects us, but the bottom line is: aren't we allowed to be the ar-
biters of our own selves—our own destinies? Isn't that the most
pure definition of freedom there is?

After Curt, despite my so-called sexual freedom, I slowly
began to hate everyone. Every person who went to college and

lived in dorms and made friends and smoked pot and talked about politics with passion and conviction; every person who got drunk, kissed a lover, and threw up as a simple and sincere right of passage; every child who was asked, "What kind of ice cream do you want?" My mother had her hand so far up my ass that I felt like a crazed puppet—frantic, wild haired, and screaming, "I should be happy! Look at all I have! I should be happy!" and wasn't. I told my mom about my depression in the hopes that she would back off the shopping and start acting like a normal mother. I really should have known better.

"There is something wrong with you, Kate. I think you need a good shrink to deal with your father issues. You don't know how good you've got it. Don't mess this all up. Get some help." Negotiation was not an option.

I began to explore what New York had to offer in "alternative paths to happiness" for those who can't wrap their mind around the joy of having money. I attended lectures on "A Course in Miracles" at Town Hall, where Marianne Williamson, a smart Jewish girl, promised that Jesus was alive and well and really gave a shit. I listened to Eric Butterworth (old white guy) at Lincoln Center's Alice Tully Hall (old white institution) prescribe methodologies for thinking happy thoughts. I bought crystals, got Rolfed, had my chakras balanced (my lower chakra, I was told, had totally collapsed), was given a free lesson in tantric sex, climbed the Red Rocks, meditated on "Ley lines" in Arizona, danced at a drum circle, sat with a triangle on my head, and tried a threesome with a real American Indian and his wife (she wasn't into it. It was weird.) You couldn't say I wasn't trying.

The ideas were cool, but the people were not. Every group had somebody in it that made me feel judged in some way, as if I weren't capable of wearing the triangle on my head correctly because I was an actress on a soap opera and therefore, "What could I possibly know?"

I finally gave in and hired myself a shrink.

Dr. May Jackson Easter's office was on the Upper West Side in the West 90's and filled with African tribal art: paintings and carvings of black men and women dancing, playing music, and looking poignantly sad. I wondered what this woman from another planet could do for me—a young, screwed-up white girl from Southern California, dressed all in black.

That day she told me something from the book, *Anna Karenina*.

"Happy families are all alike, but every unhappy family is unhappy in its own way."

Tolstoy was a pretty perceptive dude, clearly, but I don't agree. I think there is more commonality within unhappy families than he gave us credit for. I now believe that what was "different" about my family is what is common in all families who suffer internal emotional conflicts: when it is most important to have safety and security from our most intimate of relationships, we do not connect on the most fundamental level. Instead we duck and thrust and parry, like sword fighters in a pirate picture, thinking the fun is in the game but it's not.

I bought another journal and named it:

My Dreams.

I want to be free, whatever that means. I want to be happy.

I want to travel all over the world. I want to fly in a hot air balloon. I want to do work that makes me feel good. I want to go to college. I want to be normal. I want to have friends who like me because they like me and not because I am on television. I want to learn how to cook. I want to fall in love and be outrageously happy. I want a nice family. I want to feel better. I want to be an artist, a writer, a painter, and a burlesque dancer. I want to feel beautiful and drive a cool little car. I want to be free. I want to be loved. I want to be left alone.

So I left Dr. Easter, and on the recommendation of an actress friend got a new shrink—an Italian named Ron Panvini. Ron was a nice looking, soft-bodied, ex-musician in his 40's who had a curious collection of small pigs placed delicately around his office. I walked in and schlumped down on his big brown futon sofa underneath a giant poster of a man rowing a rhinoceros in a small wooden boat across a gray sea. The title on the poster read "E la Nave Va" (And the Ship Sails On.) I paid and talked. He listened. I liked this. He was funny, and although he used his pinky finger a lot to gesture, he took me seriously. He became kind of a father figure but not really. I didn't love going to therapy, but I knew I needed it. I needed to talk.

Boy did I. I talked and screamed and occasionally hit the sofa with a bat. I remember telling him everything about my mother, my father, my sister, my childhood, and my job but still, I doubted he could really help me. When I hit things, I screamed so hard I burst blood vessels around my eyes.

I told him that I felt like I was being overly theatrical.

"I feel like I'm doing some kind of Chekhov play," I said one day after a big cry.

"No," he said, "You are doing McClain."

I thought I had some idea of what I had wanted my life to be. If I hadn't had to take care of my mom, I would've lived in some super eco-friendly house in Big Sur where I would write poetry, have drum circles, smoke a lot of pot, and never wear a bra. I thought I would make love in the woods, blow glass, and maybe even be a world-class orgy priestess. I thought I would travel the world, believe what the tarot card readers said, put flowers in my hair, have strong thighs and hands and never get anything as horrific as cancer. Instead, I ended up planting my life in a city, clinging to jobs that made money so I could figure out that my deepest, most romantic dreams for myself were based on some middle-aged man's pot-saturated fantasy from a 1970's Playboy spread.

"Oh my god, I don't even have my own fantasies," I thought and sank further into a state of hopelessness. "I'm a brainless puppet. I don't even know what I want, or what I like!"

I didn't realize this was a revelation.

Thus began the era of 12-Step Meetings.

I had heard of these "anonymous" meetings where people could talk about their problems for free with other like-minded individuals. I tried them all, figuring something had to keep me alive between two sessions a week with my shrink. There was Alcoholics Anonymous (AA), Overeaters Anonymous (OA), Al-Anon (for people affected by another person's drinking), Adult Children of Alcoholics (ACOA), Co-Dependents Anonymous

(CODA), SLA (Sex and Love Anonymous), and Narcotics Anonymous (NA), which I went to once just for the hell of it. They turned out to be far more interesting than I thought they would be. After attendance at a few meetings, I became convinced I must be 1/4th alcoholic, 1/4th child of an alcoholic, 1/4th food abuser, and 1/4th drug abuser (that is if laxatives counted) because the welcoming, nodding heads, and friendships that came with my walking in the door to any of these meetings seemed to qualify me for instant membership. It felt nice to belong somewhere other than work.

"How much worse could it get?" I thought, and began daily attendance, helping myself to the free coffee, cookies, and advice from total strangers.

I liked AA meetings the best because they seemed to cover all issues under one roof. Even if I didn't really have a problem with alcohol at the moment, I could always point back to what I felt was growing into a problem back in my high school days. All I had to do was stop drinking and "count days," which was awkward but not awful. Instead of having a drink to "take the edge off," I went to a meeting. There, the honesty of the people who shared their private agonies gave me a sense of being understood. I wasn't the only one who had been raised around madness.

It felt like I suddenly belonged to a secret sub-culture. People in meetings could swear, scream, or admit to horrible behavior, and then go on with their day without being judged by anyone in the room. We were all sinners, all of us equal. We didn't even have to believe in God—just a "Higher Power" of our choosing. "Women Only" meetings held confidences with cool knowing. As fall turned to winter, I wrapped myself up in scarves, hats, and old sweaters, looking like nothing less than a giant bag of Salvation Army giveaways. When I vented my frustration about my mother, some of the women nodded their heads, gently patting me on the back as they handed me a piece of paper with their first name, phone number, and "call anytime" written on it.

I learned snappy little slogans that sometimes really helped. I could try to live life "One Day at a Time." I could "Keep it Simple" or not. I could tell myself "Easy Does It," and not worry about how I was rapidly gaining weight as I slowly began to give up my laxative and enema regime. I could "Let Go or Be Dragged," or put "First Things First," to get through one more day of not knowing who I was in a world where everyone seemed to be convinced of the absolute opposite.

Based on the growing sense of identity these meetings began to give me, I decided to leave my jewel box of an apartment and move downtown. The apartment I chose was an illegal sublet on the border between Chelsea (what I occasionally referred to as "the Gay White Way") and the West Village. In 1994, the corner of 14th Street and 7th Avenue was an odd address for anyone. A no-man's land of old wig stores and donut shops, Christian literature storefronts, and possibly the filthiest McDonald's in New York, it was just a place to buy a donut and a bad cup of coffee before jumping on the express train to get the hell out of there. I chose that particular spot because it was a world worn down by the faded hope of one generation and propped up by the ambition of the next—perfectly reflecting the tangle of my internal life. It was also only three stops on the red 1-2-3 line underneath my building to the Upper West Side, where my TV job told me what to say, how to dress, and who to be. I refused to allow anyone to help me decorate this place. Instead I spent nights shoving the antiques from room to room to decide where I liked them best. I didn't care about the scratches on the floors or the chips in the walls that the heavy furniture made. They were my scratches, my chips—imperfections that defined my liberation.

I was so excited about my new apartment. I couldn't wait to pick up the phone and tell my friend—a girl I met in AA who I have decided to call "Banana" because she always made me laugh with her crazy stories.

Banana was a bodacious blonde who liked sex more than anyone I had ever known. She had already been sober for a few years after getting thrown out the window by her coke dealer. She figured, like lots of people in AA do, that as long as she wasn't drinking or doing drugs, she could do whatever got her through the night. The last sexual adventure story she told me had something to do with a ladder, which she would hang upside down from to get the biggest rush from the orgasm. I couldn't figure out how this worked, exactly.

Banana and I liked to sit outside in the back patio at Café La Fortuna, an old coffee house on West 71st Street that catered to a niche of opera fanatics. The walls were covered with signed black and white photos of famous singers from Lincoln Center down the block. Rumor had it that it was one of John Lennon's favorite haunts when he was living around the corner at the Dakota on 72nd Street and Central Park West, but I had started going there long after his passing. It was now a common place for alcoholics to have coffee after a meeting. Coffee shops were where the real stories got told, the stuff people didn't feel safe to talk about in a large group: the abusive father, the guy they screwed over, the nitty-gritty details of an affair. If the waiter had good ears, they heard some hair-raising entertainment.

"Be careful, you're gonna bust your uterus one of these days," I joked with Banana while taking a big sip from a giant bowl of hot milk with almond syrup, "Vaginas don't grow on trees, you know."

I don't know why I considered myself so holier-than-thou. I had screwed plenty of guys. I had this delusion that I was still somehow so young that each time was another popping of the cherry. I convinced myself I was really looking for love, not just doing it for fun or distraction, so I was different.

Meet my denial.

Banana didn't talk that much. Mostly she just watched me and listened. She had the kind of eyes that made sentences. This sentence said, "You are an idiot, and you haven't dreamed of having the kind of orgasm I have, so you shouldn't judge." I knew I should stop making fun of her. Sex was serious business, and Banana was the President in Chief of the Corporation of Lovemaking.

"Thank you for your concern, Mother," Banana coolly replied, "but you really should try it. Do Kegels. And get stronger batteries for your dildo. Clearly you are needing some relaxation."

Banana dreamed of being a painter like Helen Frankenthaler and was working toward it at The Art Students League, a free-spirited place where people could take a variety of classes for a small fee. Her paintings were a passionate act of beauty and pain. I didn't feel like trying to be creative anymore. I had hit burnout. Instead, like my mom, I discovered beauty by shopping.

The windows of the Upper East Side of Manhattan are filled with beautiful clothes and jewelry, and Banana and I loved walking up and down Madison Avenue to gaze at them. We saw hand-beaded dresses made in Paris, cashmere hats with long feathers, and leopard skin shoes with bright red soles that screamed, "I have a personal car and driver and a house in the Hamptons, as well as a collection of South American lovers." I dreamt of having problems such as these.

Money didn't buy happiness, but it sure as hell paid the credit card bills. As soon as I found out what was "quality," I bought it. Although my pretty acquisitions were a lovely distraction, they didn't give me the self-esteem I hoped they would. Deep down I knew I was still a middle-class working girl without a college education—hoping that I would become someone else if only I wore the right clothes.

Banana saw me getting depressed as we walked out of Bergdorf Goodman for the five hundredth time. "C'mon, let's get out of here, Princess. Tell me about what's happening. Meet any cute guys lately?"

"God bless Banana," I thought, "She has such a way of pulling me back into the moment." I stopped considering the two thousand dollar shoes I had been ogling in the store. "There is a cute guy at work, but I don't think I'm his type. He probably thinks I'm a loser, anyway."

"Listen, you spend ninety percent of your time at work, girl. Where else are you going to meet people? Tell me about this guy. Is he nice? Is he cute?"

"Ah, Banana, he's just another big dope. He's probably got a big drinking problem if I'm attracted to him. A big dope with a big dick who is a big drunk." I longed to be wrong. I wanted to be in love and feel like I was family to somebody other than my own family.

"Maybe you're wrong, Kate. Maybe he's a good guy. You gotta give him a chance. Are you dressing cute? Why don't you invite him out with a group? Go get a coffee or something?" Banana was insistent, "C'mon, this Friday night, why not?"

I made a list of "why not's" for my friend.

"Because I work with him, because I don't know him, because he's going to say no, because I am too fat and weird and fucked up for him, because I am not normal, because I have issues, because I need a manicure, because I have too much money and he will be threatened, because my family is nuts and he will think I'm needy, because my hair's a wreck, because I am not pretty enough, smart enough, or cool enough, but MOSTLY because he will just want to get laid and I will fall in love, and he will break my heart, will ruin my life, break my shit, spend all my money, and leave me heartbroken, old and nuts—just like my dad left my mom and I don't ever, ever, ever want to feel that, that's why not."

There was a long silence while Banana took that in.

"Okay, whatever. Call him. Later. When you get home. Okay? Promise me."

I rolled my eyes and promised. Banana wouldn't take no

for an answer, so it was better to just play it off and make up some story about how he came to work with crotch rot or something so we could go back to shopping.

When I got home, I pulled the wrapping off an Angel Food cake. "Don't do it," said the Voice From Within, which I ignored. I had spent too much money that afternoon and needed to stop thinking about it and a million other things. Angel Food cake was the cure. I loved feeling its soft, pillowy texture embrace my teeth and gums, the sensation of sugar seeping into my molars, bloodstream, and brain.

"Ahhhhh," and there it was—the hit I had been looking for. One more bite, one more, and another, and maybe one more, "Oh, ohhhhh..."

I looked down at the tin foil wrapping. My God, I had eaten the entire cake—only a few crumbs of the outer layer were left.

"What the hell," I thought, and picked up the container to coax them out. I managed to get one up with my fingernail and quickly stuck it in my mouth to coax all the sweetness I could out of it. Then I chewed on the wrapper.

"You are disgusting," I mumbled to no one.

I was twenty-four. I thought about the year and a half left on my contract at *All My Children* and determined that this would be it. I would take off the girdle of responsibility to my mom and be somebody else, anybody else, anybody but somebody who had to stand in front of a camera for a living. The problem was I had now been doing it for so long I wasn't sure if there was anything else I could actually do. This thought depressed me deeply. I thought if only I could take some time off, maybe go to college, then I could find out for sure who and what I was supposed to be. But that would take Mom getting some financial help from someone other than me, and since that was unlikely, my choices were to suck it up or jump off a bridge.

The bridge was starting to look tempting.

Goodbye

Remember me when I am gone away. Gone far away into the Promised Land. When you can no more take me by the hand or I half turn to go yet turning stay. Remember me when no more day by day you tell me of our future that you planned. Simply remember me. You understand it will be too late to council then, or pray.

Yet if you should forget me for a while and afterwards remember, do not grieve. For if the darkness and corruption leave a vestige of the thoughts that once I had, better you should forget and smile, than you should remember and be sad.

~Christina Rossetti

I went to Mom and told her about my burnout.

She listened to my issues seriously, then gave me three options:

1) I could continue to keep my job, paying the rent for our house and my apartment, and suck it up.

2) She could go to work for her father in Moline, Illinois, as a secretary.

3) I could buy her a house.

The second "option" was made to sound as if it were the worst possible thing I could do to her, my "mother-who-is-dying-of-cancer-how-could-you-make-me-go-back-and-work-for-my-father-what-kind-of-daughter-are-you?" I knew I wasn't a bad daughter, or an ungrateful one. I just needed help.

Her solution for me was number three: I would buy her a house.

"It will be a good investment." She proclaimed, "I'll fix it up and you can sell it when I am dead."

I gave in. Denying her was simply not an option. After all, she had stuck with us, not abandoned us completely like our father had and that demanded endless and unquestioning loyalty. Loyalty she would test over and over again. Only a year before, with six years of cancer and treatments behind her, she had "accidentally" canceled her health insurance. This news was relayed in an evening phone call that had me dropping to the floor like Sonny Liston getting knocked out by Muhammad Ali.

"Oh Jesus God," I remember thinking, "I will never be free."

Instead of screaming at her that this one catastrophic error would cost us every dime I had saved, I said, "It's okay, Ma. I love you. I will take care of you. If I have to spend every dime I have, I will take care of you. It's only money." And I meant it. What else could I say? She was dying.

She found a house in northwest Connecticut near cow pastures and forests with a view of a lake. She planted trees and flowering bushes around the property, bought wooden blinds, curtains, rugs, and new antiques and had a fence installed. I must admit she had an incredible eye for decorating. I think in part she was trying to leave behind something she thought was valuable for me to have, like a dowry of sorts. I tried not to look at the bills. I just went to work like a good little husband and signed the checks when I came home.

She made a sweet bedroom for herself and a guest room for Annie and me. Inside her room she crammed two bookcases overflowing with art books, a beautiful antique four-poster bed, a dresser, and an antique quilt. Over her headboard was a small painting of a house in the snow. Our room contained an antique queen-sized bed with a lace cover that Annie somehow bought with her small earnings as a part-time teacher at her school. As a reward for my buying the house, I was allowed to buy myself anything I wanted. Although I occasionally splurged on shoes and jewelry, I mostly bought stuffed animals, hiding them in bags in the closet. Stuffed animals had become like spirits to me—silent witnesses to the baiting, abuse, and role switching that had been happening since I was a child.

Less than two years after I bought the house, I received a call that she was back in the hospital again. I dropped everything and raced up to Connecticut. There, my sister and I were told the cancer had moved from her ovaries to her back and her brain. There was nothing more they could do. They gave us two options: we could put her in a hospice or we could take her home. Annie checked out the hospice just to be sure, but it wasn't a real option.

I had tried to prepare for what I knew was going to be an emotional process by calling the producer of *All My Children* from the hospital and telling her what the doctor had said, but I still found myself scheduled to work five days a week. Years later I sat that producer down at a lunch and asked her why the hell she did that to me. They could have pulled back on my story easily. She told me she knew what I was going through because her mother died when she was working, and it was what she would have wanted. She thought she had done me a favor.

I would like to take this opportunity to say that if you ever have the chance to make a major decision for someone, please consider that person's situation and not your own. For five long weeks, I had to drive two-and-a-half hours up and back to that Connecticut house in an ancient Mercedes during a terrible East Coast winter after working five, twelve-hour days in a row. It pushed me to the absolute edge of my strength.

At the house, we settled our mom into a temporary hospital bed that we could elevate and lower at will. Tucked into a small space in her bedroom, the hospital bed held various clear bags of pain-killing liquids, which we could administer by pressing a button.

As I tucked her in, I wondered if my sister was thinking the same thing I was.

"Finally. Finally she is going to die and the nightmare will stop. Please, God, please, let her die soon."

Terrible. I know.

Doctors don't always tell you how long it's going to take when they send you home with a dying loved one. As it turns out, it can be quite a long process for some people. My mom turned out to be one of the few that would hang on until the bitter end. The cancer had begun in a small lump under her arm and moved into her breasts. From there it went to her neck, her lungs, her stomach, and her uterus. It was eight years from her first diagnosis until her death. Sometimes I administered the morphine when I couldn't stand watching her try to get out of bed any longer. I just stood there and pushed the button again and again, unsure if I was killing her or just keeping her still. All I knew was what the doctors told us: that she couldn't be allowed to get out of that hospital bed.

I did everything I could to make sure she experienced as beautiful a death as possible. I played an old cassette tape of acoustic guitar music we had bought ten years prior on a drive up the California coast, hoping it would remind her of happier days when the three of us were a team having an adventure together. I copied out wise words from the margins of the book *The Artist's Way* and taped them on the mirror over her bureau where she could reflect on them if she had a lucid moment. I even invited some Catholic nuns whom I had met at a nearby facility to visit with her. I read every book on religion, faith, healing, thought, and Zen—whatever I could get my hands on. The advice that stuck with me was this:

"The Wise man embraces pain, for he knows that it will teach him."

That was it. When in doubt, surrender, shut up, and listen. I found a t-shirt that said, "Surrender Dorothy!" which I thought was hilarious because I saw it in a different way than how it was meant. To me it meant, "Hey Dorothy, all your bitching ain't gonna make this any easier, might as well surrender to the inevitable." It was the only wisdom I could hang onto: accept the inevitable and it will still hurt, but it will go faster.

On the day she died, the night nurse stayed over into the afternoon. This particular nurse was a simple looking woman with a puffy face and dishwater blonde hair. Despite her unremarkable appearance, she had a grace and patience at which I marveled. The Puffy One warned us to stay near the room where my mother's bed was set up, if we couldn't wait in it. We couldn't. We had spent eight years anticipating this moment and five weeks driving up and back through snow and ice to sit and wait by her bedside. Now it felt impossible to face down what had gone from being a dreaded inevitable to an immediate moment.

Annie and I waited in separate rooms: her on the porch overlooking the frozen lake, me in the living room. We were completely unable to look at each other without getting into a fight. After an adolescence spent having it ground into us how different we were, and our young adulthood growing up faster than it was comfortable, we had become resentful and bitter strangers—connected only by the body of our mother and a history from which we both longed to distance ourselves. Little did we know, there was no place on earth we could escape from what our parents had put inside our mind.

From where I was sitting, I gazed out at a motley collection of 1970's furniture and books. Bookcases covered every wall in the house and were filled to overflowing. I thought about reading every book she owned and wondered if that would help me understand her more. The wooden coffee table in front of me was long and narrow and reminded me of being a seven-year-old sitting in front of it playing a board game while I sneakily wiped my boogers into the brown carpet. It was so heavily shellacked that I could see my own reflection in it. I looked like shit. My hair was short and colored some hideous light brown. I had dyed it a few months prior for a screen test for one of Peter Jackson's first films—a ridiculous comic horror movie with Michael J. Fox called *The Frighteners*. The casting director had told me Jackson had a thing for girls with black hair, but the soap would have flipped out if I died it that dark, so hideous brown it was. I didn't get the part. A girl with jet-black hair did.

Underneath the center of the coffee table hid a compartment. The two doors to the compartment were held closed by magnets that clicked whenever they were pulled open or closed. Inside, board games and puzzles waited to be played with—long unused relics of my childhood. I used my foot to open and close the doors, making the magnet "click" while I waited for the nurse to call out for us. I vacillated between trying to imagine what my mother's life was like when she bought this two-hundred-pound piece of shit and what kind of axe would be appropriate for the surface once she was gone. Right when I was imagining burning the whole house down, the Puffy One called out, "It's time." Words I had been longing to hear, but when they came, I did not want to go into that room.

Annie took one side of the bed and I took the other. I let my sister do the talking that day because she was the eldest, and it felt like the most respectful thing to do.

She said, "It's okay, Little Mama, you can go now. It's okay." She spoke so gently it was as if she were talking to a small child. In a way she was.

My mother's passing was, unlike her life, undramatic. There was a very slight rattle of air leaving her lungs, then no inhale. She simply stopped. Her soul slipped right out and away leaving behind nothing but a disastrous wreck of body. I was struck by how attached I was to it—this body that I knew so well.

It was a body we had fought with and fought for—a body that had been our womb, our home, our responsibility, and our only consistency. I had taken this body to the hospital to have its lungs drained. I had helped this body into a wheelchair and pushed it through an Ivy League campus when my sister finally accepted her PhD. I had bought clothes and furniture for this body, had held this body's hand, and made it drinks when it cried. I had prayed for this body to get well, read it passages from poetry books, held this body's purse when it was at the doctor's office, and put on its shoes after.

Now her giant bald body lay there like a big baby dead from a heroin overdose.

But it was more than the death of her body—it was also the death of all chances for understanding and love; all possibility words could be said that would heal; all opportunity to laugh again together over something stupid. There would be no more mother to drive us around, drive us to succeed, drive us crazy. I would never again taste her sickness in the back of my throat, smell her sweat tinged with chemicals, touch her elegant, spotted hands, or hear the tenderness that could sometimes ache in her voice. There would be no mother to lean against and wonder with, no one to help us remember what we were once like when we were small and defenseless, no one to torture us with her depression, her cruelty, her humor, or her needs.

Unable to look anymore, I walked out of the bedroom and sat back down by the hideous coffee table, girding myself for what I had been warned by my shrink would be a heavy-duty eruption of emotion. I thought I had prepared myself for this moment by hanging on to my mantra of "Surrender Dorothy" so that whatever grief did come, it would pass quickly. It did not.

I felt it first in my heart—a total sense of shattering—and then my stomach dropped out from under me and my bowels started to shake. My throat closed up and I felt like I was choking until I suddenly realized I was screaming. I found myself rocking back and forth, screaming and doubling over, howling as if my guts were being physically ripped out of my body. Annie was back again on the other side of the house, feeling just as lost, just as broken as me. We could not bear each other's company at this moment. It was too hard to look into that mirror.

Those fun-filled emotions returned again an hour later with an unexpected gusto when the tallest man I'd ever seen appeared from the funeral home to carry our mother's body out of the house. I couldn't believe what I was seeing: Mom smothered inside a thick black plastic bag, thrown like a sack of potatoes over this giant's shoulder, as he wedged her through the front door of the house I had bought for her. This image pushed me past the limit of my self-control, and I screamed like a savage under attack. I could have burned down the house in that moment. Sometimes I wish I had followed through on that impulse. My life would have been far simpler.

She did not leave a will. She had joked that she wanted to be put in her Mercedes and driven into the lake outside the house, but clearly that wasn't going to happen. She had done her best by labeling envelopes with locks of her hair and jewelry in them, reading us poems, and making sure we both had careers we could follow. She had forgotten only one thing: our entire worlds had been wrapped around her. Freedom was a concept I did not understand. Fun was what other people had the luxury of enjoying. Now that she was dead, neither my sister nor I felt what we had hoped to feel—that we could finally live as we chose. It would just be life without Dana. Wide open nothingness.

Impediments

W e had decided on cremation but very little else. We hadn't even bought a tombstone. We told the funeral home to just put her in a can, a cookie jar, or whatever came easy, and we'd figure it out later. It would turn out to be much, much later. Unable to convince Annie to come back to the house to properly bury her, I wrapped the can full of our mother's ashes in a car blanket and placed them in the front seat of her Mercedes. It sat in the garage for ten years until Annie could face the task of spreading her ashes with me.

Our father was still alive, but he had taken off long ago into his disease of alcoholism and selfishness. Since our mother's relatives hadn't been any tangible part of our upbringing, Annie and I felt they hadn't earned the right to be decision makers in the process of her death. In some respects, I don't think we made all the right choices. We forgot to give any of her clothes to the funeral home, for example. We forgot they were going to embalm her before they cremated her and that we had chosen to have a viewing of the body. We had forgotten to order flowers. We forgot a lot.

When we walked into the large "presenting room," to see her for the last time, she was laid out on a high table wearing only her hospital gown, barefoot. There was no minister, no family, no friends, no casket—just my sister and me and our mother's dead body lying on a table in a hospital gown. I saw some aging flowers that had been hastily stuck into one corner and silently thanked whatever kind soul had offered up their leftover buds of softness for strangers.

I decided this time I would do the talking. At first I wasn't sure what to say. I sat close to her and looked at her beautiful, thin hands, mysteriously and awkwardly folded. Her lips and eyes had been glued shut. She looked alive, but not really. I hated the idea of someone fussing over her dead body's bits and pieces, moving her around, poking at her. I should have at least remembered to give them her purple coat, some stockings, and the black leather shoes she liked, the ones with the gold buckles. I should have at least thought to order flowers, get a gravestone, or ask her friends to come for this day, but I hadn't done any of those things. I had only been able to get her through her death. That was the best I could do. I tried to remind myself that I was only twenty-five, but it wasn't much comfort.

I lightly touched her cold cheeks.

"Hi, Mom. I'm so sorry we forgot your coat." The guilt was crushing. I felt as if I had let her down, terribly. "We love you, Mom. We always have and always will. I hope you will remember that."

But what could she remember now? She was an inanimate object, frozen in time. There was no "mother" there. She couldn't hear me. We had paid good money to have a false second more with her as some kind of giant doll, riddled with scars and empty of life. She would now forever be what she always was—abusive, messy, guilt inducing, controlling, invasive, selfish, wildly intelligent and creative, rebellious, hilarious, and completely helpless. I couldn't stand that I hadn't been given more time to fix it, for either one of us to grow up a bit and be better for one another, for us to learn to love each other as we were and not as we wished we had been. The last year of her life she had learned to let me go a little bit, and I had learned to have more compassion for her. Why couldn't we have had just a little more time?

At least Annie was there. This day of all days we were desperately trying to be compassionate toward each other, but it was hard to connect after so many years of being played against one another. We held hands and cried heavily once again over the utter awfulness of it all. I do recall that before we drove home, my sister and I shared a couple morbid jokes— something about the funeral director and what he did with all those dead bodies in private, I think. We were both grateful for the laugh.

As I got into my car and drove away from it all, I noticed a bit of blue peeking through the clouds, which eased the look of the winter trees covered in ice and made them sparkle. Out of nowhere, a tiny bit of a sonnet popped into my head, which was hardly surprising, given all my training as an actor, but it did surprise me because of its content.

Let us not to the marriage of true minds admit impediments.

I wrote it down quickly when I got home. Where had that

come from? I hadn't remembered memorizing it, nor was I deep into Shakespeare at the time, quite the contrary. I dug into a book in the living room and looked it up. It was Sonnet 116, first published in 1609:

> *Let me not to the marriage of true minds*
> *Admit impediments. Love is not love*
> *Which alters when it alteration finds,*
> *Or bends with the remover to remove:*
> *Oh no! It is an ever-fixed mark,*
> *That looks on tempests and is never shaken;*
> *It is the star to every wandering bark,*
> *Whose worth's unknown, although his height be taken.*
> *Love's not time's fool, though rosy lips and cheeks*
> *Within its bending sickle's compass come;*
> *Love alters not with his brief hours and weeks,*
> *But bears it out even to the edge of doom.*
> *If this be error and upon me proved,*
> *I never writ, nor no man ever loved.*

A few years after she died, the strangest thing happened. Bereft, I went to see a "spiritual healer" a dear friend had recommended, a friend that was a little bit ditzy, but whom I trusted. Running late, I jumped into a cab and told the driver to take me to an address on the Uptown of Manhattan.

Inside the cab was silent. I felt so alone. My sister had moved to California for a job, and my boyfriend at the time was yet another jerk. I felt like there was no one around who could understand what I was going through—no one who wanted to hear about my pain.

Suddenly I felt my mother take my hand. I know this sounds bizarre, but I don't know how else to describe it. It was a soft feeling, not an actual physical hand, but I knew what I felt. I looked over to the other side of the backseat of the cab and saw nothing. I looked at my hand. Nothing. There was no one there, but at the same time, there was a presence.

I said, "Mom?" and heard nothing.

I left my hand open, trying to feel it again, but the feeling had slipped away as quickly as it had come. I knew she had been there. I could still feel her presence.

Then it occurred to me: she did not want me talking to this healer. I don't know how I knew that, but I did. She didn't like her.

I shook my head. Mom was being overprotective from beyond the grave.

Inside the apartment of the "spiritual healer," it was a comedy of errors. The table on which I was lying collapsed. The fax machine wouldn't stop going off. A light bulb in the room popped. I almost started laughing. Mom was not being subtle. The "healer" said she'd never felt such a wild energy in the room before.

I thought, "Meet my mom."

In order to get out of there, I told the lady that whatever I was feeling was probably my dad's fault, and I yelled a couple times to give her the idea that I had a release. I would have done almost anything to get out of there. My excuses seemed to be satisfactory because after I blamed my dad, all my mom's energy left the room.

My head spinning, I paid the lady and left. I decided to

go on a walk to process what had just happened. I had wanted her spirit to visit me for years, but this…this was so strange, and now I couldn't feel her at all. After walking a mile or so, I looked up and found myself on Madison Avenue, near a store that sold fancy women's clothing—Barney's.

"What the hell, I'll go shopping," I decided. "Distract myself."

Just past the front doors on the main floor of Barney's department store is the section where they display jewelry—some of the most creative and expensive jewelry in New York. I was enjoying looking (and not buying) when something caught my eye. It was a silver bracelet with the tiniest writing on it I had ever seen—so small I couldn't even read it from a foot away. I had this strong feeling, however, that it said something I needed to read.

I called the salesperson over to show it to me.

He pulled out the bracelet with a salesperson-y smirk and handed it over so I could take a look. I could not believe what was written there.

Let us not to the marriage of true minds admit impediments.

Hello, Ma.

Freedom Is Expensive

fter her death, I moved from the illegal sublet on
Seventh Avenue to a new apartment on Ninth Avenue
and 14th Street. (I had to move. The building's owners
found out I didn't hold the original lease and kicked me out.)
This was years before the fancy restaurants and clubs took over
and the area, known as the Meatpacking District, still smelled
like the blood of the animals that were being cut into pieces
there—blood that ran constantly into the cobblestone streets.
It was considered an unsafe neighborhood, but I didn't care.
It had character. Safe from the smell in my new apartment,
I would sit in a chair and look out the window, watching the
transsexual prostitutes go on the beat and gay men stumble
in and out of the local S&M club, "J's Hangout." I once heard
there was a baby pool inside where guys could stand naked
while a fat, old woman sat in a cage, laughing at them. The human carnage was a great distraction until my mind started to
turn on itself—pulling up memories I could do nothing about.

There were several ways I have considered killing myself:
taking pills, cutting my wrists with razor blades, jumping off a

bridge, and throwing myself in front of the subway all seemed like strong contenders. Never hanging, though. That seemed too violent. Slitting my wrists in the bathtub always felt like the one I would ultimately go with. Since I found out the Romans used to off themselves that way, it seemed the coolest. I'd have to write a hell of a note to apologize to whoever found me because what a sight that would be, and the smell, oh yuck. That thought is what stopped me from going the distance. I didn't want to be a burden to anyone—not the way my mom was to me. Plus it seemed so pathetic. It was just relief I was looking for: relief from pain, worry, heartache, pressure, exhaustion, and more than anything—memory.

Sitting in the window watching the men below debase themselves, a voice started whispering things like, "Deep down no one really cares about anyone," and, "Your presence in anyone's life is a burden relieved only by anticipating and satisfying their needs. Dad's here. Better be nice, better behave, or he will go away, and you will never have his love or protection. Do what Mom says, or she'll get angry and yell and hit you or worse, ignore you or make you sit in the car while she drives like a madwoman. Ask for what you need when she can't be bothered and become the silent witness and unmeaning instigator of some unknown source of rage that always lingered beneath her surface and it will be your fault—your fault for making her mad, for awakening the monster inside her, your fault for everything hurtful she says or does because if you had only stayed quiet, if you had only needed nothing, then you wouldn't have gotten hurt."

I had to put my head down to fight the tidal wave of nausea that was beginning to overwhelm me.

The voice in my head became vicious, "Can't leave, can't stay. Always pain, always strain between the people who were supposed to love you but really only dreamt of getting away from you—their baby, their little needy screaming, hungry child."

I heard my shrink saying, "Your parents did not love you."

Hello, razor blades.

"FUCK THIS!" I shouted to no one in particular, "FUCK THIS SHIT!"

I knew at some point, things would be different. At some point, a day would feel good again, food would taste fresh, and life would feel like a series of happy possibilities instead of shocking occurrences. At some point there would be no more yelling in my head. No more hurtful words with edges that cut. No more wasted youth.

I just needed to beat the shit out of a few people first.

I thought back to six months after our mom died, when I flew out west so Annie and I could see our dad again. He had moved all over the country but now lived in the city where he had been born, oddly enough. Annie wasn't so sure she wanted to see him, but I thought it was important for us to at least face him after all that time.

We met at a restaurant.

His smooth hands sat unmoving on the polished dark wood of the table. Behind him I noticed the walls of the restaurant glowing softly in the early evening light. Curtains of gold, orange, and yellow created an almost circus-like atmosphere. I could hear laughter, bright and innocent, emanating from the other customers. I doubted they could imagine that at the table across the room, two young women were meeting their father again, seeing his face and hearing his voice for the first time in fourteen years.

He wasn't alone. A woman sat beside him glistening with a light sweat. He was no longer with the secretary. I had no idea why this one was no nervous. It wasn't her reunion. Annoyed, I decided to break the tension.

"So," I felt the professional actor rise up, taking over my personality, "Where are you living these days?"

I barely recognized his tiny voice. "I'm with Sue. We live up the street."

Sue wore nice rings and good makeup. She was poured into tight, pretty clothes that looked expensive. I suddenly realized she was presenting herself like she was going to be our "new mommy." Aghast, I decided if she spoke, I was going to stab her with my fork like a whale hunter would—mercilessly and without emotion.

In order to keep Sue silent, I talked about Mom's cancer, and how it eventually killed her, all the while closely watching our father's face for a flicker of grief. I saw none. It was a blank. For a moment, I wondered if he were really my father. I was hard pressed to see any resemblance between us whatsoever.

"Oh, I'm sorry," he said, looking down.

Sue put a hand on his arm and glared at us as if we had just tried to murder him. I stared right back. He wasn't ashamed enough. Not for me, anyway. My sister was even harder than I was. She just sat there and emanated hatred for him. I remember wishing she would soften, just a little, so we could get through the conversation a tiny bit more smoothly, but she didn't. She came because I had asked her to—not to forgive.

"And...are you still a lawyer?" I tried to posit this question gently. I was trying to give him his chance, his opportunity to regale us with his sad journey across the nation, his remarriage and divorce, his tragic addiction to alcohol and drugs. I waited what felt like minutes for him to respond, my mind open to, well, perhaps not complete forgiveness, but acceptance that could soften in time to something like affection, given the right circumstances.

"Yes, I have an office nearby, too," he said. And that was it.

My mind went blank. All our years of sacrifice and struggle passed through my mind in rapid succession. My eyes searched for a place on the table. I was looking for some thought that would force this moment into making sense. I couldn't stop thinking of all the years that had passed with no child support, no phone calls, not one letter. He didn't seem to notice.

"Ah ... " I said.

I had "Love thy Parents" burned into my brain with a branding iron at the horse ranch I attended as a child. It was God's Law. God had to have made that law for a reason.

My eyes caught the gray sheen of his too-good suit. I was suddenly startled by how foolish he looked. His beautiful suit was a mockery of his failures as a man. Then I noticed he wore silver and gold cuff links and a gold wedding ring. I was sure he had on Italian dress shoes. I was wearing a black sweater from The Gap. My sister shopped at Filenes Basement. Our mother was cremated in her hospital gown. Every dime I had made in my life had gone toward taking care of my family. Where was his guilt—his sense of failed responsibility? All I had wanted to hear him say was, "I am so sorry," or maybe even, "Let me do what I can to help you now," or possibly even, "I want to see you whenever you want to see me."

Instead he asked, "How do you like your job?"

Stunned, I shrugged, "Um, uh... It's fine. Hard work."

"Are you still teaching?" he asked my sister.

I shook my head. He was talking to us like we were his clients not his children—the children he had bought Christmas presents and dolls for and then so casually abandoned all those years ago. Sue squeezed his hand, as if this were All So Hard For Him. I bet he hadn't yet told her he spent every dime I made as a child actress.

I bet not.

I couldn't understand how I could be related to this man, this wet fish with such flimsy, useless hands. I had quit high school at sixteen to fight my way through the world and provide for my mom, my sister, and myself. I refused to stand in line for welfare. I had pride. Where was that quality in him? Where was his pride? If we were family, why couldn't I tell?

I knew he was a recovering alcoholic. In the culture of AA this meant that lots of things were not "his fault." He had a disease, of which he was a victim. I was prepared for this. I was prepared to understand. But this was his moment to step up and admit the damage he had done. Somehow, he hadn't quite seemed to grasp the need for it.

I looked again at the woman seated next to him. She was rich. That was it. She was taking care of him, enabling him to indulge in the role as victim of his life and, like my mother, propping up his ego with her faith in his potential. It didn't take a rocket scientist to realize he was still a con artist, living off this poor woman's charity and good will.

It made me sick to my stomach.

In that moment I swore I would never take a dime from anybody. Ever. Then I promised myself that if he ever asked me for money, I would cut off all contact and never speak to him again.

Five years after we saw him, Sue kicked him out. He called me and asked for $5,000 and the Mercedes.

"Just something to get me back on my feet," he begged.

I told him that I had finished paying for that car when I was fourteen. I told him he could pull himself together and go get himself a damn job, like I had. Then I hung up and sobbed my guts out because I knew I would never speak to him again. He had forced my hand. I had made myself a solemn promise never to speak to him again if he asked for money, and I was a woman of my word.

For better or worse, I do not draw lines in the sand lightly.

He died five years after that, from ALS brought on by alcoholism.

When I was back in New York, I dreamt again that I was riding that big black horse—only I wasn't going into the cave, I was flying. My hair blew back over my shoulders, out into a dark blue night sky, covered with stars. My body was slim and

lithe, my legs gripped to the body of the horse as if we were
one muscle, connected at the bone. Shooting stars flew past
my head, and I blinked away the tears that started to gather
in my eyes from the dust. I had to ride harder, faster. Had to
move forward, away, and quickly. The joy in the escape rippled
through my body, pounding in my ears, my guts.

"Don't be afraid," said a voice from somewhere, "Learn to
be free."

"Who was that?" I said to no one. It sounded slightly like
my mother's voice, but how could that be? My mom would
never say anything like that, not the mother I knew.

There was no reply. Typical.

I started to think about my dad. Would he have said
something like that? I doubted it.

I got up because I felt myself drooling. The pillow was wet
from my saliva and had created a little puddle of wetness there.

"Ugh, how disgusting," I said aloud. I pulled myself out
of the creaky antique bed and slipped on some comfy socks.
As each lover came and went, the bed had grown creakier
and creakier. I was surprised nothing had snapped yet under
the weight of it all. "Good old 18th century craftsmanship," I
mumbled, stumbling to the kitchen and putting the kettle on as
I contemplated the miracle of its dowels—wooden pegs that are
made to fit perfectly into holes in order to hold together a bed
or table. "Nails are not dowels," I concluded, "Nails just hurt.
I need something like dowels to hold me together. Something
strong, like big wooden dowels."

I thought about writing a book about my lovers. I had
started with an idea for the title, "They Came and They Left, a

Contemplation of Cunning Linguists," which made me snort as I put milk in a pan next to the kettle. Something about the idea still appealed to me, but I was intimidated by the idea of other people imagining my vagina.

I took my coffee with hot milk to the window to take a peek outside. It was too quiet that morning. I missed the sounds I had grown to become fond of—taxis honking, yells from delivery people getting out of their trucks, the rush of cars going by as the world went about its business. New York was always full of movement, commerce, industry, and acquisition. This harshness kept things real and kept me in the moment. This was important because now that I had internalized my mother's voice, it had become pushy and loud, randomly piping in when triggered, which for some bizarre reason seemed to happen a lot when I went grocery shopping.

"Get the Mallomars," came the voice.

"I don't want Mallomars, Mom. I don't like Mallomars."

"I want Mallomars," the voice insisted, "Maaaallloooom- mmmaaaarsssss..."

"No Mallomars, Ma!" I started to feel vaguely nauseous and wondered if I was saying something aloud.

I feel a sharp WHACK inside my head.

"Mallomars, you bitch! For all I did for you, you can get me a goddamn box of Mallomars!" Her ghost arm flipped up like a quick fish out of the water and smacked me in the face.

"Don't be afraid," was what the dream voice had said. "Learn to be free." Whose voice was THAT? I wasn't even sure what "free" was—what that meant. Free to travel? Free to make art? Free to study? Free to have sex? Every man I was with seemed to want to help me find "freedom" with my ass in the air, and then proceed to tell me how I should and shouldn't act or what I should and shouldn't do with my life.

"Is freedom love?" I shook my head. I knew some men knew how to love deeply, but they didn't want to be possessed, and most got bored once possessing me fully. I either irritated them with my "issues," or they became so possessive I felt trapped. "Men are hunters," I thought. "Can't argue with nature. Some women might like that, but that's not freedom for me."

I knew some men were different—that they could be both gracious and strong. I had seen them on television. This awareness that there were good men in the world gave me some solace, but the ones I knew seemed to want an extended adolescence. They were "Peter Pans," forever running from responsibility, leaving it to some "Wendy" to clean up their mess. Don't get me wrong: I knew women who were like this, too. They drove me nuts. This wanton stupidity, I decided, was a version of what some adults called "holding onto their innocence," but really felt like a stubborn denial of anything that made a person an adult human being worth knowing.

"So in fact," I reasoned, "no adult can be innocent because by a certain age, you really should know something about life and how to behave, and if you don't, then you are just willingly ignorant. And willingly ignorant is not innocent. Willingly ignorant just makes you an asshole."

"Are children assholes then?" I wondered, feeling philosophical, "Perhaps unwilling mini-assholes?" I thought this was a fair question. Was part of the joy of childhood this undeniable right to be a total jerk, and that was what I missed out on—a refusal to accommodate anyone else but myself? Was being a child the experience of demanding my way? Insisting my needs be met when I had no strength, no wisdom, nothing more going for me but youth, my dreams, and the fact I existed?

Perhaps this was the secret. Innocence meant denial. Innocence meant righteousness. Innocence meant absurdity in the face of tragedy.

I soothed myself with milky coffee and this new thought, "Children are savages who are only curtailed in their greed by consequence. Children are easily manipulated. Children need more than they give. Children are not really free because they rely on adults to take care of them."

I felt some pity for them and a tiny bit for myself.

"My parents acted like children. But this should not exempt them from consequence because adults have had the benefit of time and experience and should know better. My parents should have known better. They should have stopped invading me with their wants and needs and thoughts and hands and dicks and tubes of hot water."

I made a vow that from here on out, because I, at twenty-five, had taken the time to find out what adults were SUPPOSED to know—that I would tell many, many more people to go fuck themselves.

I had more thinking to do first. The dream was still bothering me. "Learn to be free..." What did that mean?

"Is freedom money?" I wondered aloud. Mom had taught me New York meant options, and by "options," she meant opportunities for making money. Everyone in New York knew this. It was an implicit, unspoken understanding. Money could buy friends, respect, even forgiveness to an extent. It explained everyone's heartache and everyone's triumph. If people were smart, they made money. If they were stupid, they didn't. This thought made me feel very bitter about the world, but at least I knew I could make my way through it now. I could work at the job I struggled with to make the money I needed to buy my freedom. I would take what was offered and buy myself an education, a wardrobe, an apartment, and a life. Sacrifice and reward. The Carrot and the Stick. The last thing I had wanted.

No, money was not freedom. It was a trap. It was a trap I couldn't let go of, and it was fear that did this to me. Fear and the ghost arm.

I took out a jewelry bag full of rings my mom had once bought me from the consignment stores in Connecticut. All semi-precious stones: rubies, sapphires, garnets—nothing really large enough or fine enough to be very valuable, but not small enough to waste on daily wear. I put one on each finger as far as it would go and sat on my velvet sofa, wrapping my arms around my body to feel the warmth of beautiful things. I only felt myself. There was no one to hug me and tell me that it would be okay—no one to "fall back on." No one to demand that I take care of them, no one to force me to make choices, no one who relied on me, no one to wake up to who would ask me how I was, or what I needed.

I put my hands over my face and began to cry. Large, guttural sobs bursting out from behind my bejeweled hands. I was finally alone—free to do what I wanted, when I wanted, but all I wanted was another chance at being a child, so I could grow up right, maybe get all the pieces inside me connected in a better way. I couldn't be a child without my mom. I needed more time to get her approval, her friendship, more time to grow with her, forgive her.

But she was dead, and money would not buy back her life or my innocence.

I went to my bed and pulled the blankets up as far as I could, crying hard into the soggy pillow that had been my wake-up buddy, letting the pain of all the loss burn me up like a paper in a fire, until there was no more. Coughing and sputtering, gagging into a Kleenex, I finally took myself to the toilet because I thought I was going to barf. It was too much for me, this freedom. Snot rags were everywhere. Tears and drool dotted the 800 count Calvin Klein cotton sheets. I suddenly felt a little pee stain in my underwear from the force of my crying, and I laughed out loud for the first time in weeks.

"Oh the humanity! Look at me! I'm a mess! Okay move, Kate, move, move, MOVE..."

I took off the rings and placed them by the side of my bed thinking how silly and tragic I must have looked a moment ago, curled up next to the toilet like a glittering snail.

"Get dressed, get out. Just get outside. Fresh air, yes. Breathe." I threw open the closet like a drag queen and began to rummage. "Put on something colorful, sexy, grab kookiness, go for comfort. DO IT. Red blouse, black tights, blue jean mini skirt, striped socks, yes, big black sweater, scarf, floppy hat, boots, big bag. Fill bag with notebook, books, pens, phone, keys, lipstick, and glasses. Get out the door. Call somebody. Go to bookstore. Get coffee. Do ANYTHING, just GET OUT OF THIS

PLACE AND WALK. MOVE!"

I left the ghost arm on the bed. There would be time to slap myself in the face later. That day freedom had to mean saying yes to the moment I was alive in, right now. It had to mean embracing hope. It had to mean believing that there was a place in this world for a girl who could fly through the night sky on a big black horse. I knew I had to move harder, faster. I could not allow myself to be caught by fear. Hooves clamored on the lightning bolts in my mind, but I decided not to listen to them. I had to decide that there was something in me that could not ever be touched, something that would never be broken. I had to decide that I would fight for myself like no one had ever fought for me—aggressively, like my mother hacked at the statue my father gave her with her axe. I would hack at my fear, my feelings of unworthiness, and my loneliness. I would do this because although I was now no longer innocent and could never be again, I owed it to myself to remember that, once upon a time, I was.

Epilogue Shmepilogue

As for the question, "What is freedom?"

As a teenager, I began to think about freedom in the usual way—escape from my mother—but I had the added responsibility of taking care of her. My existence then was defined by taking care of others. "Freedom" meant only having to care for myself. The problem was you have to have been taken care of in order to know how to take care of yourself. You have to be taught how to do it. Because my parents didn't know how to take care of themselves, they couldn't teach me how to take care of myself.

I looked to relationships, money, work...all the things I had experienced in life to try and take care of myself, thinking that it would give me a sense of freedom. I couldn't shake this idea I had that some people simply felt FREE.

In AA there is a saying, "We will know a new freedom and a new happiness." I was hooked by that. I did experience some freedom and happiness there, for sure. The camaraderie of those who came together was indeed fulfilling for a time, and to not look to substances or experiences for answers, but to look to a higher source for joy was also a very important lesson for me. However, that organization wasn't able to deal with all the issues I had.

I had to dig deeper.

I discovered I was trapped in the past by the trauma I had experienced, and that the only way to get to freedom was to look deeply into what happened and come to terms with it. Writing this book has been a huge part of dealing with everything that happened to me. A very painful way to do it, but I had to wrangle it out for myself. Creativity has always been a compelling pathway for me. Looking at the words I have written over and over again has helped me know more about how I feel and what I need to let go of—over and over again. It has helped me have more compassion for my parents and to see them as people with their own painful pasts, not just as my "mom" and "dad." Through writing, I am no longer a victim of circumstance but someone who claims her experience. I can say, "I lived through this" without confusion or apology.

I also have developed relationships with professionals that could simulate parental relationships for me. I needed caring, connection, and real parental love. Two therapists became like a "good mother" and a "good father" to me. I saw Ron for ten years, and Colette for five. I am still in touch with her and even saw Ron for coffee when I was in New York a while ago. I dedicated myself to not hating men, and by developing a non-sexual relationship with a father figure like Ron, I experienced what I should have gotten from my dad. Colette became a caring, good mother figure—someone I could trust to not hurt me or react when I said how I felt.

I also began to cultivate my own "inner good mother." Sometimes I pretend I am talking to a little old wise lady who completely loves and accepts me. I ask her about stuff that is worrying me. Then I pretend I am her and tell the worried young person what I think would be good advice. It usually comes down to simple words: "worry less," "love more," and "joke 'em if they can't take a fuck."

(I know the last one makes no sense, but it always cracks me up.)

Now I have a new therapist here in L.A., and she has an amazing technique. She always focuses on the positive aspects of an experience. She points out my resilience, my desire to look within, and my willingness to try other ways of living. She keeps in the forefront of our conversation the fact that I am a good person who is allowed to FEEL good about myself. Perhaps this positivity is more endemic on the West Coast, but I couldn't care less. I used to feel that to be self-confident meant you were filled with an obnoxious ego, and as much as I sometimes admired people like that, I felt it was distasteful. Now I think that true self-confidence is important because when it is clean and coming from a good place, it can inspire you to strive to help others and make the world a better place.

Finally, it is so important to me to keep connected with my sense of God. I don't define God in any specific way. There are too many gorgeous religions in the world. I can walk into any temple and feel connected, even if that temple is the top of a mountain. What matters is that I regularly acknowledge that there is "something" that exists, both within me and around me in all living things, and that I honor that "something." I don't even call it "God" much of the time. I don't really have a name for it. It's an energy. If you pressed me, I would call it "The Great Mystery." It's such a personal experience. It grounds me in our shared human experience, making it meaningful.

I still believe there is a self inside us that cannot be broken. The awareness of this self within doesn't always spring to everyone naturally. One has to go looking for it, hunting it down like a mushroom in the forest. I call it "The Inviolate Self." This identity can and will take care of our wounded inner child, our broken teenager, or our betrayed adult—even if we are mentally ill. The Inviolate Self is made of pure compassion—compassion turned inward. It is a self that allows us to get help because we have decided we are worth helping.

This is very different, in my opinion, than the spirit. The spirit is that part of a person that is connected to something greater than our little minds and bodies. In my opinion, the spirit within a human being can be a rather fragile affair. Once wounded, it can retreat into its essence, waiting like a tiny seed for conditions that signal it is safe to blossom. Tragic life experiences can kill someone's connection to his or her spirit, and thereby their willingness to live.

I don't believe that a willingness to live need be connected to our ego. The ego is attached to a part of our human will to survive. It does this by competing to win and working hard. However, I think people want to live because it feels good to be loved, because nature blows us away with its magnificence and makes us wonder about the great beyond—not because we've conquered the world or have millions of dollars in the bank. When we see dolphins being mass slaughtered, hear stories of people killing women and children, or watch our skies covered with smog and pollutants, it dampens our belief in the goodness of mankind and the world, lowers our hope for the future, and wounds our spirit. In order to have hope, we need to feel some kind of trust, some kind of belief in something, or someone.

Adults from abusive homes do not easily trust others. We are very sensitive to criticism and have little confidence in ourselves. Our internal world generally vacillates between despair and rage. Joy peeks out sometimes with the help of alcohol or drugs, but it's not a real joy—it's a simulated one. It is a joy that can only exist because something is blocking the pain. Even in that state of manufactured aliveness, we are easily influenced by the ideas of others. We feel like freaks. We fear our own needs. We look to others: lovers, husbands, children, to help us change our lives or ourselves, and when they cannot we despair. We cannot fix the past and we cannot move forward with confidence in our own lives. It's a soul sickness that is passed down generation after generation, a crushing emptiness that dooms us to feel hopeless instead of fulfilled. We turn to fantasy. We turn to creature comforts. We turn to drugs, sex, food, alcohol, or shopping. We turn to cults. We will do anything to escape the sorrow of what we lost before we were aware of what we should have had.

I think what we need—what consoles those of us who were damaged by life so young—is a daily living proof of innocence. Children are the sacred holders of the spirit of innocence, but so are dogs, cats, horses, and other animals. I suppose one could say that even plants have an innocent energy to them as they are living things—blameless, pure, and uncorrupted in their intent.

It is a fact that children can endure, but only so much. A wounded adult can break a young person's spirit. I've seen it done. That's why wounded adults need to take their pain seriously. The children of traumatized parents can be smothered in their parents' hopelessness until they cannot dream of a better world. Their whole being becomes consumed with the idea there is no way out, no safe place—and they snap. The children of Holocaust survivors, for example, are often plagued by the same nightmares that haunt their parents. They can grow up to be traumatized, depressed adults, despite the fact they didn't see, feel, or experience any of the terrors their parents witnessed. It is a fact that more than stories are passed on. Terror and its bedfellows—demoralization, shame, trauma, and depression—can be passed from father to son, mother to daughter.

I am so happy that I didn't kill myself. If I had not taken the help given, I would have missed out on the amazing experiences I am having now. I would have missed marrying an incredible man who is the blessing of my adult life. I would have missed laughing and spending time with my sister—our healed relationship now full of silliness and acceptance for who we are and what we both survived. I would have missed the joy of loving two fabulous dogs, whose innocence and loyalty touches me every day. I would also have missed the great joy I feel working again as an actor—my focus purely on the pleasure of the experience of acting for its own sake.

Now I have both pity and compassion for my parents. I

even forgive them. I can do this because I recognize they simply did not know how to love any better than they did. The only difference between my parents and myself is that I decided I wanted to be happy more than I wanted to be right. I decided to face my fears and change as soon as I realized I could live a different way. I realized that although what happened to me as a child wasn't my fault, it was now my responsibility. The madness of dysfunction was going to stop with me.

My newest therapist brought up an interesting point recently. She said, "We still don't know why some people are resilient and others aren't. What makes some people able to survive difficulties in their lives, even thrive despite them? It's as if certain people just choose that they can and will do something, so they do it. You know what I mean?"

All I could say was, "Yes."

Photos

Young Dad in love

Young Mom in love

Mom and me, the year I was born

Mom and Dad and Annie (Mom graduates from Law School)

Photos

Dad hug

Third grade

At home

Annie and me

Photos

Guinness Book of World Records

Backstage on *Pennies from Heaven*

My first professional headshot, by Jorjette

On the set of *My Favorite Year*

Photos

Horse ranch

Prom and perm

Mom painting

Sophomore year

Photos

Mom as usual

Mom painting at the apartment on
Riverside Drive, Los Angeles,
California

Cross country trip

Cross country trip

Photos

Minskoff Studios, New York City

Studio apartment, New York City

Dixie begins

Cady McClain

My headshot, photo by Ron Rinaldi

Photos

Emmy win with Michael E.
Knight

Michael E. Knight

My first apartment

Mom and me

Photos

Mom

Sheared like a lamb

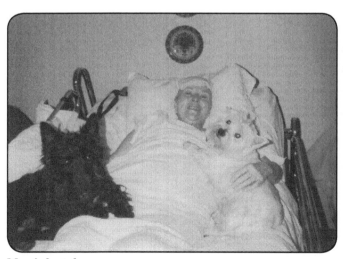

Mom's last days

Acknowledgements

First and foremost, I must thank my first two therapists, both of whom spent years with me: Ron Panvini and Colette Dowling. Without their love and guidance I would most certainly be dead.

I must also thank my husband, Jon Lindstrom, who shows me every day what real love is, and who sees me not as a collection of my experiences, but who I am in spite of them. Enormous thanks go to my dear sister, who gave me her permission to let our story out into the world. I've tried my best to honor and protect her. She deserves only the best.

This book would not be possible without the warmth and friendship of my friend "Banana" over twenty-some-odd years.

I am also so grateful to the poet and writer Davyne Verstandig, who encouraged me to keep writing, despite the pain.

Thanks go also to Leanna Brunner for all her help in making this dream of a book into a reality, as well as Erika K. Rupp, Lisa Jey Davis, Joe Masi, Deven DeMarco, Matt Rozsa, and Vivian Gundaker—all of whom read my book at various stages and gave me essential insights and encouragement.

Finally, I want to thank the many anonymous people I met in twelve-step programs who gave me their support and taught me new ways of living. You know who you are. You saved my life.

Sources for Help

"The Artist's Way" by Julia Cameron

"The Language of Letting Go" and "Co-dependant No More" by Melody Beattie

"Courage to Change: One Day at a Time in Al-Anon II"

"The Twelve Steps for Adult Children" by Friends in Recovery

Al-Anon Hotline: 1-800-344-2666

Alcohol/Drug Abuse Hotline: 1-800-662-HELP

National Domestic Violence Hotline: 1-800-799-7233

To learn more about how PTSD (Post Traumatic Stress Disorder) could be affecting you, and to seek out sources for help, check out The Sidran Institute for Traumatic Stress Education and Advocacy (www.sidran.org) or The Trauma Center (www. traumacenter.org).

Made in the USA
Lexington, KY
17 June 2014